Talk about your Oxford...

John P. Moir

Published by John Moir

© Copyright John Moir 2012

ISBN 978 0 9573910 0 0

Printed in Sandwich, Kent

"Talk about your Oxford,
Pretty little Oxford Town,
I could walk you up and down
If you'd just follow me round....."

PROLOGUE

Why bother to put all this down on paper? Partly because I am tired of relating some of the episodes and prefer to look forward rather than back. Partly because these were experiences at a time in one's life when one had the energy, fitness and time to do whatever one pleased. Partly, perhaps, because I discern signs in our national psyche which lead me to believe that such opportunities may not last for ever. Already, as I write, there are the products of a less complete education who have arrived at University full of resentment and unappreciative of the possibilities which it offers. They prefer to destroy rather than to use.

Certainly, Oxford and Cambridge are unique. When I consider the lives led by the students in continental universities, they seem narrow by comparison. There is, first of all, a general inability on the part of the students to organise themselves in order to pursue their own interests. There are fewer clubs and societies and those that exist have minimum activities. The idea of running cooperative stables or a pack of hounds would be classed as fantasy. Nor is the actual system of teaching the same in foreign universities. The institution of the tutorial, the crux of the Oxford and Cambridge system, is entirely lacking. Instead, the students attend lectures with several hundred others, or maybe a translation class of fifty. It is difficult to see how a spark of genuine interest can be encouraged under such circumstances, nor can this system teach one to enquire and question, which is the basis of scholarship. Instead, as at school, marks are gained for repetition. The system is not helped by the fact that anyone with an Abitur or Baccalauréat qualifies for entry to University – the weeding out of the unfit taking place as much as seven years later when degrees are failed. This seems a callous waste of the most energetic stage in young people's lives. At Oxford and Cambridge, the weeding out is done at the start and only those with certain chances of a degree are allowed to enter.

However, we appear to be moving towards the continental system in Britain too, in an age which does not appreciate the value of true education either personally or for the country as a whole. It is an age in which the state gives all and the individual is deprived of all responsibility for foresight and effort. When one considers the eagerness with which nations on the make grasp the opportunities of training and education the shadow of Imperial Decline looms uncomfortably large.

There is, of course, implicit in my thesis the philosophy of working hard and playing hard. With organisation, the day is never too short. This is perhaps the basis of English public school life - keep them busy and they do not have time to get up to any mischief — and of course the institutions are complementary. At University, however, nothing is arranged for you, which is disconcerting at first, but then the school system has taught one to stand independently long before one's contemporaries abroad. It is therefore a time to establish one's own tastes and pattern of life.

The colleges themselves aid and abet this. Each undergraduate had his own, or shared with one other, a set of rooms, often panelled, and a servant, who woke one in the morning and acted as a general valet. One had all the services of a first class hotel or a good Officer's Mess. It was, for example, possible to give private dinner parties in one's rooms. I remember one I gave with Turtle soup, salmon, pheasant, bombe surprise and savoury, accompanied by several wines and the college port and served by the butler and two scouts, which came out at less than £1 per head. Such a thing would be unthinkable in any continental university. But the traditions were long established. Those rooms had been occupied before me by Sir Thomas More and Sir Walter Raleigh.

Oriel was a small and friendly college, which had probably reached its greatest period of distinction just over a century before as the home of the Oxford Movement. While I was there it achieved some distinction by coming Head of the river, an event which was celebrated in the traditional manner by burning a boat in the front Quad and a celebratory dinner in Hall. During this, festivities got somewhat out of hand and a beer mug was thrown through a full length portrait of Queen Anne, ancient Visitor of the College. The immediate reaction was regret, which soon turned to delight when the picture came back repaired and cleaned, which process revealed a further six inches of engaging décolleté painted over by our prurient grandfathers.

The whole of my time was not spent in College. For my last year I lived out in a farm cottage on the outskirts of Oxford, with Bertie Boyd from Univ. now making his fortune in Hong Kong and Gavin Tweedie, of the House and the Royal Horse Guards.

I would not pretend for a moment that everybody at Oxford led similar lives to those of myself and my friends. Everyone was free to lead the sort of life they wished. But at least the opportunities were there to make use of it if one wished. One might counter that not everyone had the financial resources to do as they wished, but I would query that. My father gave me an allowance of two hundred and fifty pounds a year, which was not a great deal. My father also paid my tuition and accommodation fees, which would have otherwise been covered by government grant. I added to this by joining the Territorial Army and doing an enormous amount of training every year, which I thoroughly enjoyed. Apart from this I used to change my old motor cars fairly frequently, usually at a profit. Finally, there was the minimum government student's grant of £50 per annum, which went straight into my equitation fund. Frankly, I believe that many Undergraduates from less privileged backgrounds had greater financial resources than myself, and also spent more, frittering it away on beer in pubs.

I certainly looked forward to going up to Oxford. Since leaving the freedom and sanity of the Dragon School it was my earnest desire to shorten my public school career as much as possible and to take the first opportunity of entry to University. Thus I resisted the offers to stay on an extra year and take a scholarship to Oxford. There followed a curious interregnum of nine months. I went to the University of Vienna for five months in a rather spurious capacity to improve my German, worked for a month as a hospital porter to earn some money and finally spent two months on a small island in the Orkneys shooting rabbits, watching birds and seals and rolling silage.

On rereading the events described it seems extraordinary that they should have taken place as recently as the late 1960's. Perhaps that is why I bothered to take up my pen.
CHARLBURY, 1974

CONTENTS

CHAPTER ONE

MODERN PENTATHLON

Among the many new experiences and ideas which may have confused the undergraduate at the start of his career at Oxford, there was an institution which shone out like a guiding light in the storm. This was the Fresher's Fair, which allowed the new undergraduate to get some immediate order into his recreational life. At the start of every academic year all the many and varied university Societies combined to hold a good imitation of a North American Association Convention in the Town Hall at the top of St Aldates. Each Society or Club would erect a booth in one of the two large rooms on the first floor of this imitation late rococo building, whose impressive marble staircase and first floor were a monument to civic pride and the epitome of all that was finest in late 1920's cinema architecture. The freshman thus had the chance to talk at first hand with members and officials of these Societies and to make his choice between the Cricket and Tennis Clubs, International Trotskyists and the Conservative Association, Ramblers and Archaeologists, Explorers and Existentialists. There was a staggering variety and the ultimate choice probably ran to three figures.

The freshman's fair of 1965 was to have a profound effect on my whole career at Oxford, since one thing was to lead inexorably to another. I suppose that even before I started to mount that fine staircase, with all its promise of dimly lit double seats at the back of the dress circle, my fate had been sealed.

"You're just the sort of fellow we're looking for!" cried a familiar voice while I was still several steps short of the top.

The Oxford University Modern Pentathlon Association, better known as 'Oumpah', had seized a strategic pitch at the top of the stairs and framed in a dazzling array of the tools of trade - spurs, pistols, running shoes, Olympic swimmer's skull caps and sabres — was Mike Wood, who had been my captain of fencing and of swimming at school, the only events in which I ever achieved any degree of enthusiasm or proficiency.

"Come off it Mike, you know damn well I'm not a sporty bastard" I countered, relapsing into the standard defence of school years. But it was no good, like a Jehovah's Witness with his foot in the front door, Mike sniffed a convert. He slipped an automatic pistol into my left hand and a biro into my right and my name and College was on their list.

I had never been able to summon up much interest in the normal team sports which the English educational system has to offer. Since the age of six at the Dragon School, I had played them all; hockey I quite enjoyed whenever my massive swipes at the gallop actually connected with the ball, and rugger was tolerable for someone of my weight and build so long as I played wing-forward and before they changed the rules and prevented me nipping round to snatch the ball at the back of the scrum, or if this was not possible, at least sitting down hard on the opposing scrum half as he tried to remove the ball from the scrum. Cricket was the worst of the lot, the idlest and most boring game that was ever conceived. I remember years later going for an interview for a job and the first question was:

"Do you play cricket?"

"No, I loathe the game" was the immediate reply

"Pity" came the rejoinder, "I find a love of cricket indicates a tolerant character"

No Job!

As far as sport is concerned I prefer more active and more individual sports. I fenced foil and some sabre for the colts team at school until I damaged my hamstrings through lack of proper fitness and warming up, and had spent most of the early part of my life in or on the River Cherwell, leading Upper II A to triumph in the Dragon School Regatta in my final term. At Tonbridge I swam backstroke and some freestyle for the school.

Mike Wood knew his stuff. Modern Pentathlon demands a compact frame and an individual spirit, for there is no-one to compete with but yourself. A sense of balance and quick reactions are important for fencing and for riding, and a cool nerve for pistol shooting. After that there are two types: the swimmers and the runners. It is rare that one comes across someone who can do each equally well, largely because two different physiques are required. For the runner, long deep lungs and a calmer disposition. For the swimmer high lungs capable of short but massive intakes of breath, a lot of weight on the shoulders and the spirit to go in and knock hell out of the water. Of the two it is easier to recruit the proven swimmer, since swimming is in large part a matter of technique and physical conformation, which can be improved on only marginally, whereas with a big enough stick behind them and a great deal of determination most people can be made to run.

* * *

And so it was that I started training. At times, there were as many as fifteen or sixteen of us, but about a dozen were serious. We fenced in a hall at the back of Woolworths, we ran at South Park, Headington, two or three circuits up and down Headington Hill, we shot at the old TA barracks at Cutteslowe. Swimming was a problem and we fitted in between public sessions at the Temple Cowley baths and the small St Edward's School pool, but swimming facilities at Oxford were abysmal. Riding was an even greater problem and one which we never solved, all of the local establishments proving unsatisfactory. Cambridge certainly had better facilities than we did and all our efforts were ultimately directed at beating them in the Varsity match during the Easter term. The best training sessions were the matches themselves and most Saturdays we went off to measure ourselves against Durham and Cambridge Universities, various Army teams and Sandhurst, the Navy and the Gloucester Club which included two members of the British Team, the Phelps brothers. It was during the Navy championships that I managed to beat the British Champion, Sgt Fox, at Epée. I played a blocking game, which is the only option open to the weaker fencer, parrying his every move and waiting for his impatience to grow and for him to make a mistake or take a chance. It paid off and at my final point he tore off his mask, cried out in rage and hurled his mask down the other end of the hall. I don't blame him at all.

Another feature of that match was a visit with Tony Temple to my cousins near Okehampton. We had a splendid evening and tanked up right royally, so much so that when we drove back in my 1946 MGTC to the barracks at Plymouth the sentry stopped the car at the gates and asked me what its registration number was. I regret that I was unable to help him on that one.

We rose at 5.30 a.m. the next morning feeling very weak and went out to the running course for the start at 7 a.m. It was cold and very windy. The Navy had chosen a bleak cliff and headland for the course, the last land which Sir Francis Drake saw when he too set out to do the impossible a few years previously. I rated running well below cricket and as we walked the course my heart sank as we came to the bottom of hundreds of feet of cliff, up which part of the course led. There must, however, be a moral in this somewhere, for the result of an immoderate evening the previous night and a stomach full of bread that morning was an improvement of two minutes off my usual running time, a feat never equalled before or since. The beneficial effects of alcohol in relaxing muscles for the shooting even were well known, although none of us ever tried it. Shortly before, at a major championship in Switzerland, one of the members of an East European team achieved a very high score, only to cap it by shooting through a Swiss policeman's toe and collapsing in some nearby bushes afterwards. Breathalysers were introduced after that. I did once give myself a fright in the shooting event when waiting for the targets to come up, holding the pistol in prescribed manner down my right leg. Unfortunately, my finger brushed the trigger and it fired in that position. Having heard that when shot the blow isn't always felt straightaway, I could not be sure that I had not shot myself. Very slowly I gathered the courage to look down, expecting to see a shattered kneecap or a mangled foot. The bullet had grazed my right shoe and taken out a piece of concrete the size of a half crown beside it. I tried not to make the same mistake again.

As the end of my first term approached, it became evident that I had a good chance of making the team for the Varsity match next term. The prospect of a Blue with two terms of arriving at Oxford was a powerful carrot. Already modern Pentathlon training was taking almost every afternoon every day of the week. I put myself into an accelerated training programme over the Christmas vac. I did not miss a day's training, mostly running, my weakest event. On Christmas Day morning I went for a run through the University Parks and up the path on the Marston side of the river. It was bitterly cold and there were flooded fields all along. The river was in full spate. As I ran further the flood water on the path came up to my ankles. Then up to my knees. Finally, I reached the Victoria Arms at Marston Ferry, and asked the landlord to take me across on the ferry, as he was obliged to do. He refused. I pointed out the difficulties in returning the way I had come. With a fine sense of Christmas spirit he still refused. I announced my intention of going across on the wire. I was about a quarter of the way across the wire, flat on my stomach, in best commando style, when a voice boomed out on the bank I had just left.

" - That's the last time you'll be doing that Sir, I've called the Police to pick you up on the other side."

I looked round to see the landlord and the entire complement of the public bar watching my performance. It was very slow progress and already my stomach was inches underwater on the slack wire. "Sod this" I thought and took to the water. There was an extremely strong current flowing in the winter floods and needless to say, on Christmas morning it was shockingly cold. I struck out for the bank and realised that my only hope was a quick sprint before my muscles froze completely in the cold and I was swept downstream. I pulled myself out on the other side and with a fine gesture at the crowd continued on my way. (Nowadays a new road links North Oxford and Headington.)

* * *

It paid off. Mike Wood, last year's captain, dropped himself from the team and I was in, on condition that I did two rounds of Christchurch meadows every morning before breakfast in addition to the normal training. The date of the match had been fixed long in advance. The only cloud on the horizon were my preliminary examinations.

The Oxford system works roughly as follows. Undergraduates are selected on an entrance examination which is supposed to gauge their ability to get a good second class honours degree at the end of three years. It is a test of potential and originality of thought. The preliminary examination, which takes place in one's second term, is a further test of ability, set now in the context of new subjects, or a new breadth of syllabus in the original subjects, and also, more importantly in the context of a free University environment rather than the strictly supervised atmosphere of school. It is essential to pass this examination and it is possible in a case of really poor performance or gross idleness to be thrown out first time, although usually one has two chances. The exams are taken very seriously and many people's Oxford careers have terminated abruptly after one year. It was therefore a matter of some concern to learn that the dates of my preliminary examinations were to coincide with the first day of the Varsity Pentathlon match. There was little I could do until the actual times of the papers were announced. When they were, it was the knell of doom. A paper in the morning and in the afternoon. I went to see the Dean of my college to ask whether it would be possible to sit the papers earlier or later and to pass the day in strict supervision. The Dean replied that this was out of the question. My heart sunk, however, I had underestimated the man. I had overlooked the fact that he had an England Soccer Cap, having played goal for the country. His suggestion was extraordinary and comparable only to a Royal Pardon for a condemned man.

" - It is impossible to alter the times of the exams. However, you must not miss this chance of getting a Blue. If the worst comes to the worst, you should ignore the preliminary examinations this term and take them next term instead. And pass!"

This was great news, but I thought there might just be a chance to play bowls and beat the Spaniard as well. In the event I shot at 8 a.m. in sub fusc, ate a hearty breakfast, went into the exam at 9 a.m., walking out an hour early with an alpha on the paper, although I did not know it at the time. I had arranged a sports car to be waiting with engine running at the main door of the examination schools. We drove at breakneck speed up to Cowley baths, where the swimming event had already started, throwing off sub fusc on the way. Almost as soon as the car stopped, I dived into the pool. After lunch another exam, and at 5 p.m. the fencing event. After that a low key party for the Cambridge team, an early night, a good sleep and the running event, followed in the afternoon by the riding. Both these events were in Blenheim Park, the former on a course fixed some weeks previously by Robert Coate up three steep hills and through a stream. To his horror, he realised nearer the time that he was going to be in the team and it was too late to alter the severity of the course he had planned.

For the riding, I was loaned a splendid horse called Freddie, appropriately the name of the current Grand National Winner, by the Duke's agent Major Murdock, and Freddie took me round in a flash with one fault to bring us in the easy winners of the event. Unfortunately, after we passed the end of the course and I pulled him up he crossed his front legs and stumbled. I flew off between his ears and a moment later Freddie collapsed fair and square on top of me. Some bystanders pulled him off me but as he got up he used my back as a footrest. By this stage, I was, in fact late for another concurrent exam, my first exam in the OTC for a commission. As soon as Freddie was clear and I was changed, I drove off to Dartmoor for a night exercise which I joined about midnight. It was bitterly cold and we did not have, as was always the case with the old T.A., the proper equipment. We really froze; my water bottle froze solid and so did several of our weapons. I had the bazooka, which played a prominent part in a scholarly display of fire and movement in a dawn counter attack. That night, in spite of all the excitement and lack of sleep, I did not get much rest as Freddie's hooves were beginning to make themselves felt. I reported sick next morning and spent the day being x-rayed and manipulated in Barnstaple General Hospital. To my disgust, I had to sit through the passing out parade at the edge of the parade ground.

* * *

Most of the University sporting clubs had an annual dinner and towards the end of my first summer term, Oumpah met for theirs. It took place on a fine summer evening in the Alington rooms of University College and as we went in to dinner the sun was lowing and its rose coloured rays filtered through the leaden window panes onto the carved panelling of the room. Outside stood the enormous mulberry tree of the fellows' garden and the dome of the Shelley memorial which I passed many times as a child in the High Street and had thought must be some kind of early astronomical observatory. The Univ. Chef put on a superb meal and at the end of the summer term with examinations and the Varsity match behind us, we were in relaxed and carefree mood. Conversation was general and towards the end of the meal I was talking with Prince Alexander Galitzine on my left about Russia before the revolution, prompted by the film "Dr Zhivago", currently showing at the Moulin Rouge cinema. The port appeared and I turned to my left.

"Come on Konky" I said, "let's drink it back as in Russia!"

We stood up as one person, drained the glasses and staring straight ahead, flung them over our shoulders. The glasses crashed against the beautiful panelling and broke into tiny pieces. There were cheers, encores and slapping of hands on the table. The butler must have been the model P. G. Woodhouse had in mind for Jeeves. Neither he nor the rest of the staff batted an eyelid. In a flash two new glasses were put in front of us and filled. We repeated the performance amidst further cheers and again new glasses were brought and filled without question. I dimly remember someone else on the table trying the same trick but alas he had imbibed immoderately. His glass drained, he did not remain upright long enough to hurl it over his shoulder, but instead sank silently, first to his knees, then slowly out of sight under the table.

We adjourned for coffee and liqueurs to a room on the top floor between the first and second quads of Univ. A certain amount of horseplay of the 'Mess Games' variety developed. I remember everybody somersaulting over a table, I managed it once but the second time forgot to put down a brandy glass which I was holding and while I was upside down over the table it crushed in my hand. I didn't feel anything at the time or later, but bits of glass kept emerging from my hand for months.

At about this time somebody noticed that an open air performance of "Androcles and the Lion" was going on in the quad below. From our birds eye view, we could see backstage, the stage and the audience. Mike Jack opened the window and playfully pointed a fire extinguisher out. For the first time, I will now admit that in a state of slightly impaired judgement, I then playfully kicked the charger of the fire extinguisher. Mike was left holding the thing as it poured out its foam all over the stage and a large part of the audience in the quad thirty feet below.

We all thought this a tremendous joke and the audience clearly thought likewise. The Univ. Dean caught a fair proportion of the foam and we heard later that two American tourists in the audience said that it had made their visit to Oxford to be at the centre of a merry undergraduate jape. Not everyone found it amusing however, and we looked out of the door to see Androcles, the Lion and a motley collection of semi-naked slaves, gladiators and toga-clad Romans rushing up the stairs howling for our blood, laurel wreaths flying and the play temporarily abandoned. It would at that moment have been imprudent to open the door and plead reason. Eventually the Dean and the College porter placated the mob, and soothsayers, emperor, romans, and the countrymen returned to the stage.

We were granted safe conduct out of the front quad and repaired for further diversions to another part of the college and a further set of rooms. Outside these rooms was a flat roof upon which we disported ourselves until a military member produced a thunderflash. After this had been lit, the problem was where to throw it and an open window about five feet above the roof seems the obvious choice. Almost at once there was a blinding flash inside this room and a tremendous explosion. Smoke billowed forth out of the window and as it cleared a little, a small black naked figure appeared, choking and gasping for air. It was Salim, who had a reputation for pulling birds, so it was only a matter of time before a larger, naked blonde girl stuck her head out of the window gasping for breath. It transpired later that they had been rather actively involved at the time and the force of the explosion simultaneously blew out the panels of the bedroom door and brought down a newly plastered ceiling in the room below.

We judged it prudent to leave Univ. at this stage and headed via New College Lane to the Turf Tavern. New College Lane is very narrow and as a Mini appeared at speed we linked arms across the road. It gave no sign of stopping for us so we walked straight over the top of it. The driver got out, put a hand to his forehead and grasped his car for support. At the Turf were some drunk people from Brasenose celebrating their Headship of the River and consequent Bump supper. Most were past help, staggering in and out of an ornamental pond and falling off their chairs. We left for a game of cards in the Turl and as we passed the Radcliffe Camera, Mike Jack was seized with an uncontrollable urge to climb it. We advised against, but he would not be stopped. The Camera at this time was encased in scaffolding for cleaning, for otherwise it was a notoriously difficult climb, especially when one came to the overhanging cornice, several undergraduates having fallen to their deaths attempting it, before night climbing, along with the habit of stealing policeman's helmets, mercifully passed out of fashion. It was an amazing sight to see Mike, having had a fair quantity to drink during the course of the evening, climb up the scaffolding in his tails and white tie, go over the top of the roof and down the other side. After a few rounds of whatever it was we were playing I felt that it was time to retire and I returned to my rooms in Oriel Street. While I was in the bathroom I fell over backwards into the bath and much to my dismay found it impossible in my weakened state to get out of the bath. I must have made quite a noise as I remember the rest of the house crowding at the door laughing at my unsuccessful struggles until mercifully, Lethe-wards I sunk.

CHAPTER TWO

HUNTIN' AND RACIN'

One thing led to another. At the first meeting of Oumpah I met Chris Marriott, then Master of the University Pack of Draghounds. This was a marvellous institution entirely financed and run by undergraduates. There was about eight couple of foxhounds kennelled at Garsington along with the University Pack of Beagles. The venture was financed by individual subscriptions, the point-to-point, hunt balls, dog shows, jumble sales and so on.

The Draghounds gave a substantial grant to the beagles each year and somehow ends were made to meet. Independent of the kennels, we also ran our own stables at Middleton Park near Bicester, renting the vacant stableyard of the Lutyens house. To help in these ventures we employed a kennelman at Garsington and two stable girls at Middleton. The kennelman was dedicated and stayed for years but the stable girls were always a problem, mainly because we were unable to provide suitable accommodation for them. If they left, as they often did, we all had to share the work and drive out from Oxford several times a day to look after the horses. There were usually about a dozen horses kept — private hunters and point to pointers in the winter and then when these were turned out to grass in the spring, their places were taken by the polo ponies.

Chris proposed that I should come out with the Drag on a hireling the next week and I readily agreed. I had ridden in a far from serious way since I was six, at first accompanying one of my older sisters on Port Meadow when she was going through the horsey stage and later while I was at school, mainly as a legitimate means of getting off the premises of a school which I did not much care for and which I found petty and constricting after the fine common-sense of the Dragon. I hadn't ever jumped anything bigger than an oil drum though, and no more of those than can be counted on the fingers of one hand.

I should perhaps explain what draghunting is all about. A day's foxhunting proper can vary a great deal. Some days hounds will run several times and twenty miles might be covered at high speed. On other days, when scenting conditions or the supply of foxes is less reliable, hounds may spend the day drawing crops and coverts but never run at all. The average day will probably involve half an hour's cantering or galloping, some jumping if hounds are running, according to the country, and several hours hanging about on the edge of woods or fields waiting for hounds to find. Draghunting involves no fox; but the hounds follow a 'line' or trail of aniseed mixture laid across chosen country by a runner who precedes the hunt by half an hour. The advantages for the thrusting rider are obvious — each line may take twenty minutes to gallop over, there are probably three lines per afternoon and 50 or more jumps will be arranged. The pace is naturally very fast and it has more in common with steeple chasing than foxhunting. The Oxford Drag has had a reputation for 150 years for hard riding, the pace is hot, there are plenty of five bar gates and awkward fences to jump and it is a fine test of horse, rider and the nerve of both.

I approached my first day with no small degree of trepidation. It was a joint meet at Deddington with the Cambridge Drag. Traditionally Cambridge would be immaculately turned out and most of them would have a fresh horse waiting for each new line. These were seldom needed as our pace and jumps sorted them out early on. This may sound a little biased, the Cambridge country is very flat and the jumps are well prepared and the Oxford country makes much greater demands. The Cambridge Drag does have the enviable distinction, however, of using some of its original lines established in William IV's time. The Oxford followers usually had scruffier horses and dress ranged from swallow tailed coats to jeans and sweaters, but we reckoned to finish the course and get more fun out of it too.

A hefty black horse was unboxed for me in the village square and glasses of port circulated, I had shaved with care that morning as I always have on days when I felt there was a chance I might not shave again. The familiar Cotswold stone of my native Oxfordshire, slightly reddened in this part, served to reassure me though, and I could think of no better way or place to go if my number was to come up that day. Suddenly we were trotting away down the south east corner of the square in a crisp clatter of hooves which echoed off the stone walls on either side. A gate was opened into a field on the left and we followed in and down a steep grassy hill. At the bottom was a five bar gate. The hooves were thundering now in a fast canter on the springy turf. This was the moment of truth. I aimed at the gate, twitched my spurs and seemed to be looking up - not down - at the top bar. Suddenly, we were over. Not very beautifully over, but over and away the other side. I could do it. A wave of relief and exhilaration shot through me. And over we went for the rest of the afternoon. I came off once or twice, I fell behind the field once, but I finished and as we trotted home at the end, I knew it was in my blood for ever.

Henceforward horses were to take up a large proportion of my time at Oxford. For three years I hunted, dragged and played polo. I exercised, looked after the sick and the healthy and schooled the wayward. I was learning avidly all the time. No one who knows anything about horses will ever claim to know everything, but I learnt a lot. Most of all I developed that hidden sense about the animals which I believe is granted to few. I came to prefer and rely on my own diagnosis and treatments rather than the vet's and I came to make sense out of most horses which came my way. It was a fine training ground, for many of the horses, both hunters and polo ponies, were 'problems', loaned or given to us by owners who could not manage them or for whom their ailments were too much trouble to look after. I never had a comfortable ride hunting for years, as I always got the 'problems', but there was no finer way to learn. An animal with no vices will teach you nothing and serve only to give the rider a false impression of his abilities. I became a subscriber to the Bicester Hunt and hunted in the vacs, so that I came to know their country as the back of my hand. Polo taught me more about controlling and aiding the horses than hunting, but those who have never played polo will never agree with me there.

Of course I made mistakes too while learning. My brother's wife loaned me a young bay mare, Newleaf. A 'problem' - a lightly built racehorse which had been in training as a hurdler. I wanted to turn it into a steeplechaser, but it had learnt to knock hurdles flat and jump with little effort. I was advised to put it at some big, solid jumps and it would learn to pick its feet up again. This was not good advice and we had some cracking falls in this manner. Newleaf's temperament was very hot and my exercising, in spite of the protests of the stable girl, who I recognise now knew more than I did, did not help it.

Finally in the middle of qualifying her for Point to Points with the Bicester we hit some iron railings and although she did not falter at the time, a splint came up on the off-fore and she went lame. I could not afford to stable a lame horse for several weeks and she went back to Somerset to be sold. I realised later that I should have entered her for amateur hurdle races instead.

Alas like languages, the knowledge of horses and that instinctive sense fades with lack of use and I wonder if it will ever come back.

*　*　*

The Drag of course provided innumerable amusing incidents. There was one meet at Eynsham Hall which had its share. One member of the field that day was a portly and pompous man who was rumored to have made a great deal of money rather quickly in property. He was evidently anxious to cut a fine figure. One of the lines ran straight through a wood to the edge of a muddy and stagnant lake, where it turned sharply right along the bank. I happened to be following behind the gentleman in question when we came to the wood and he was going at a fair speed. For some reason when the horse came to the lake it anchored on hard and I arrived just in time to see a corpulent figure, resplendent in silk top hat, tail coat and brimstone-check waistcoat describing a fine parabola over the horse's ears to land, with a gluey squelch in the mud and shallow water. He waded back blowing muddy water from an apoplectic face and elegantly draped in duckweed. Unfortunately the horse fared less well and it took us some hours to free it from the mud into which it had floundered.

Earlier that day one of the Masters had arrived in his usual conveyance, an ancient and ragged London taxi which, in a gesture of defiance at the fates, he had successfully coaxed down to the Red Sea and back. The passenger compartment was habitually crammed full of bales of hay for the horses and wedged in among these members of the hunt staff were sometimes privileged to travel. For some time the taxi had been neither licensed nor insured and many articles which the Highway Code regards as germane, such as the odd headlight and number plate, were missing. The Master of Hounds reckoned that a quick drive through the country to the seclusion of Eynsham Park was worth the slim risk of an encounter with the Law, but this meet had been arranged by one of his fellow Masters who had, playfully or otherwise, omitted to reveal to him that Eynsham Hall was now a Police Training College. The taxi rattled unsuspectingly along towards the Park and turned through the main gate in fine style and on three wheels. Sheer horror was written inches deep on the face of the driver as he counted no less than six policemen in line abreast strolling up the drive towards him, in the heart of the country. At the last minute the line parted and a trace of amusement was visible on the face of the Law as six hands saluted in unison the passage of this remarkable vehicle, whose driver crouched low and furtive over the wheel, dressed in all the finery of the chase.

* * *

Early one morning the Master came round to the rooms of about six regular followers of the Drag, asking whether we would be free to hunt that afternoon. It wasn't a normal hunting day but horses were to be provided at the meet. It was all a bit mysterious but apparently had something to do with Princess Anne and no one was to be told. Konky Galitzine and I drove out to Shotover Park, home of the Crown Equerry, Colonel John Miller. The place was full of Household Cavalry scurrying about tacking up black horses. We were clearly going to give them some cross-country experience not readily available in London. I drew a fine looking horse and asked the groom how it went.

"Fine standing for hours on end outside the Horse Guards Sir, but I expect you'll need to stick one up its back end sooner or later, Sir."

How prescient. It was one of the most reluctant jumpers I have ever met. We gathered outside the House and Princess Anne appeared with many of her Windsor Pony Club. We were there to lend a touch of local colour I suppose. We hovered discreetly in the background. At the time, the Royal Family were careful to keep well out of the controversy concerning Blood Sports, which foxhunting immediately raises in so many people's minds and psyches. Draghunting was an acceptable concession and it was not until much later, when her reputation as a rider was established, and it could be seen that foxhunting was a necessary training to enable her to compete effectively in international events, that Princess Anne began to be seen on the hunting field.

The field moved off towards one of the gates by the main A40 road. Police were already in position and halted the traffic on the dual carriageway at our approach. As I crossed I caught a glimpse out the corner of my eye of a frustrated lorry driver tearing off his cap and throwing it to the floor of his cab, all the while demonstrating his loyalty to the Crown and its entourage with a shaking fist and gestures loosely based on those of Sir Winston Churchill.

I had just finished the last line when I saw Princess Anne take a tumble at the final fence riding Doublet. She sat up rather dazed and bleeding from a broken nose. I rummaged in my pockets for my handkerchief and rode forward to offer it in the service of my country. By this time the Crown Equerry was on the scene and my offer of assistance was greeted with a sharp "Bugger Off". I then looked up and saw that the bleeding Princess was encircled by a ring of young hopefuls such as myself, all proffering handkerchiefs of varying cleanliness in perfect unison. Within three minutes the surrounding bushes had disgorged a startling number of strong-arm men in identical trilbies and mackintoshes, anxiously scanning the countryside for SMERSH or something, and an ambulance had arrived to whisk the bruised royalty away.

* * *

In my second year I was also asked to run the Bullingdon Club Point-to-Point steeplechases. I rarely turn down a challenge and this monumental piece of organisation in a completely new field was too much to resist. I planned it in advance down to the smallest detail and thoroughly enjoyed it all. The construction of the course was overseen by one of the Masters of the South Oxfordshire Hunt on whose land most of the course lay, but all the rest, advertising, schedules, racecard, catering, all facilities, car parking, bookmakers and so on were entirely up to me. We were very lucky to have a spell of fine weather so early in the season and we ended up by making twice as much money, £800, as anyone had made previously.

I will not say that there were no mishaps, but they were minor if not altogether lacking in comedy. At one stage things got pretty hectic inside my Secretary's Tent. A large, indignant and gin-sodden racehorse owner collared me and almost laid about me with her handbag for not sending her jockey a free car-pass, an item which she had failed to ask for. While this was going on a girl slipped in and started to broadcast an appeal from the microphone for "Michael Pratt, aged 4, lost in the Members bar wearing a tweed suit with short trousers". Shortly afterwards Lord Michael Pratt, a corpulent and prominent member of the

Bullingdon Club, with a complexion out of Fielding's 'Tom Jones', retaliated with an appeal to the young lady to go to her Rolls Royce in the car park where its wheels had been removed. At about the same time, a woman came into the tent, to demand whether I knew what was going on in the ladies lavatory tent. It transpired that a sharp local woman had nipped in early in the day, set up a table and chair and removed all the lavatory paper, which she was prepared to sell back to patronesses of the establishment at a very high price per sheet!

A photographer for "Jennifer's Diary", the social column of Queen Magazine, appeared and asked to know who there was to photograph. Having gratified his curiosity to some extent I sent him down to photograph the cars on the rails, describing my father, who cannot distinguish one end of a horse from the other, as a prominent European racing expert. I was amused some hours later to see this photographer hovering round my bewildered parents using up an inordinate amount of film on this scoop.

The next day William Hickey, the gossip columnist in the Daily Express, rang up to get a story.

"Now Mr Moir, about this Point-to-Point," went the whining voice on the telephone "I mean, were there any NAMES there?"

"I am afraid I don't quite know what you mean" I answered.

"Names, you know, titles, your actual aristos."

Time for a plug for one of my more picturesque but obscure friends I thought.

"Well, there was Charles Townshend" I said.

"Oh good, good." came the reply, then a pause. "Er - this Mr Townshend - er - who is he?" The voice came back, "I mean - er - is he ANYBODY?" The pleading voice went on.

"Well it is Townshend with an "H" you know" I volunteered.

"Ah!" came the deep sigh of professional relief from the other end of the telephone.

The end result of the Point-to-Point was a healthy financial position for the Drag hounds for another year, the Drag "button" and an election to the Gridiron Club. I was to eat at the Grid almost every day for two years, preferring Mrs Bowerman's savoury herring roes on toast and Mr Bowerman's cocktails to anything else in Oxford.

Later on, Robin Lane-Fox offered me the Mastership of the Drag hounds and after some reflection I reluctantly turned it down in favour of trying to do some work in my final year. As things were to turn out this noble intention was to be largely frustrated for reasons beyond my control and it has always been a matter of considerable regret to me that I never took this opportunity when it was offered.

CHAPTER THREE

POLO

During the Easter vacation each year we would prepare for the coming polo season. The polo ponies would be brought in from various farms and friends about the country where they had wintered out and to make room for them the hunters and point to pointers would be turned out to grass for the summer. Polo was run on very free and democratic lines at Oxford and was open to any member of the University who wanted to give it a try. Over the years the Club had managed to acquire up to a dozen ponies of its own and this was really the secret.

At Cambridge there were no club ponies and few people were prepared to go to the expense of buying and keeping at least two ponies of their own, unless they were assured of making the University team. The result was that there were rarely more than four people ever playing at Cambridge, whereas at Oxford there usually were about ten regular players and another half dozen or so who played from time to time. We were also most fortunate in forming part of the Kirtlington Park Polo Club, whose facilities we were able to make use of virtually free of charge due to the generosity of Alan Budgett. We therefore had plenty of people to play with and more important, plenty of readily accessible expertise to learn from.

The Kirtlington club had a very pleasant atmosphere and, being surrounded by the fine mature trees of the Park, is one of the most attractive grounds I have seen anywhere. Our stables at Middleton Stoney were about four miles away. Those of us who were really keen would buy one or two ponies of our own to supplement the club ponies, which were of varied standard. In my second year I was fortunate enough to acquire a very good grey pony called Orchid from Mrs Philip Fleming, Ian Fleming's aunt. I do not think I am being indelicate when I disclose that this remarkable lady was seventy two at the time and still hunting and playing polo. (Shortly after this, six years later, I met her out hunting with the Heythrop. She was, as usual, among the front runners. She told me that she had recently taken up driving in a big way to satisfy her energies.) What is more she was an asset on the field, since although her shots did not have great distance, they were all perfectly played with extreme accuracy. I once watched her play in a team at Kirtlington with Colonel Humphrey Guinness, who had represented Britain at Polo in the 1936 Olympics and who at the time was seventy four. Needless to add, Orchid was perfectly schooled and had been beautifully ridden all her life as a polo pony and could be completely controlled without using the reins at all, simply responding to the rider's leg movements and shifting of weight. I learnt a lot from this horse and it was possible to take her from a walk right up to a gallop and back to a complete halt, and weave in and out of trees at the same time, without any reins at all.

Running the Polo Club required a lot of time and effort. For a time I was secretary of the Club, as I had been for the Modern Pentathlon, and stable manager. There were more horses in the stables in the summer than during the winter and extra riders had to be organised every day to exercise the ponies, or to ride them over to Kirtlington and back. Polo ponies are under greater pressure than hunters and suffer more injuries and strains in playing so that they all require stricter care. Those with playing faults had to be patiently schooled and instruction had to be given to new players. Most Sundays there were matches and these were often away and transport had to be arranged. The finances of the Club were often precarious but we built them up from subscriptions, charges for the chukkas, a ball, jumble sales, raffles and so on. Expenses involved in matches fell directly on those taking part. The stock of ponies had to be maintained of course and new ones bought as horses became too old or sick to keep on. Once, things got difficult and we approached our patron, Viscount Cowdray, who kindly offered to match every pound we raised through our own efforts with a pound of his own. We appealed to old members and ran a number of sales and raffles and managed to raise £350 which put the club back on a sound footing. I remember an interview with our bank manager at this time, which was a period of economic recession involving severe restrictions of credit. He asked for security for our outstanding debts and I offered him six polo ponies. He accepted, hardly batting an eyelid. I often wonder how that branch would have coped with the animals if they had foreclosed on the deal! All the bank managers in Oxford with whom I had dealings were very understanding towards the bizarre requests which faced them from the University clubs or societies and I never heard of a bank manager being let down.

* * *

We had other difficulties too, mainly with stable girls, although their living conditions were more bearable in the summer. One Sunday morning our two girls simply walked off and were never seen again. Unfortunately there was a match away that day and we had to feed, prepare, muck out and box all the horses ourselves, and after playing the match and returning home late at night unbox, feed, and groom once again. First thing next morning I was invited to read out my essay on medieval French morphology at a group tutorial at Lady Margaret Hall, one of the girls' colleges. The girls' colleges always took a less tolerant attitude towards extra-scholastic activities and I thought that there might well be a sense of humour failure when I admitted that the essay had not made the transition from worthy intention to reality since my stable girls had walked out the morning before. We had won the match, though, if that was any consolation. At this, a smile crossed the face of the tiger and the excuse was accepted. My philology essays were not worth hearing anyway.

There was, in any case a very happy ending to this particular story. Throughout this century, when the Old Country has been in peril, in all the confusion of its senility, the young countries of the Empire have rallied squarely in its hour of need. And so it was that Chris Ashton, an Australian in the team writing a thesis on colonial attitudes in New Guinea, plumbed the depths of Kangaroo Valley and the Fulham Road and returned with three splendid Australian girls, Jan, Suzy and Viccy who did a magnificent job with the ponies for the rest of the summer.

* * *

In my last year, we went down to Taunton to play a couple of matches one weekend. We had considerable transport problems as the box we had hired broke down a day or so before the match and we were unable to locate another one at short notice. We managed to scrape together some trailers from friends around Oxford and various vehicles to pull them. Justin Cartwright, a South African writing his thesis on Cromwell's political theory, or lack of it, managed to borrow a very rickety old trailer full of holes which I was surprised to see the ponies enter at all, and a very ancient Willys jeep which must have been one of the earliest products of Roosevelt's lease-lend agreements. The jeep had no brakes to speak of and the trailer loaded with the ponies must have weighed a few tons. Now, if you look on the map at the roads between

Oxford and Taunton, you will see that Frome, in Somerset, is practically unavoidable. Frome lies at the bottom between two extremely steep hills and the road goes straight down one hill, through the town and straight up the other hill, with the help of a moderate bend. At the lowest point in the road, in the centre of the town, is a pedestrian crossing. The road as far as Frome presented no great problems for Justin, so long as he did not exceed 25 mph, kept a good distance from any vehicle in front and prepared for halts at road junctions etc., half a mile away.

Frome, however, posed insoluble problems. There was no hope whatsoever of stopping the jeep and its loaded trailer once it started to roll downhill, or even of moderating its speed in any way. A somewhat shaken Justin confessed afterwards that he had simply had to aim the jeep down the hill and pray that no one drove out from any side streets into his path, and most of all that nobody ventured onto the pedestrian crossing. The carnage that would have resulted from any collision in that little town makes me shudder to think about even now. I think it preyed on Justin all weekend since he had to repeat the experience on the way back as well.

My own trip was not uneventful either. I had arranged to borrow a trailer and Land Rover from some friends and the night before we were due to leave, I went round to pick them up only to find that the Land Rover was in Germany. I had no hope of finding another one by that stage and the same people kindly lent me their brand new Rover 2000 TC instead. This car was not even 2 weeks old and had only started its running-in. They implored me to be careful with it and I promised that I would. At eight o'clock the next morning I went out to the farm where the ponies were now stabled. I must have been half asleep still, for the car was engaged in reverse gear when I started it and before I could do anything we shot backwards into the trailer parked behind. Upon inspection the bodywork at the rear proved to have been considerably modified. After winning the final match the next day, Julian Eeley, filled with much elation and a similar quantity of whisky, drove his Land-Rover backwards across the stable yard with great accuracy straight into the front end of the Rover 2000. By now, things were a touch on the embarrassing side. I decided that if I could get the damage repaired a full disclosure of the facts would only cause bad feeling. First thing on Monday morning I took the car to a repair shop I knew and explained my predicament. When I returned at 5 p.m, they had done an extraordinarily good job on the car. I duly took the car back at the appointed time. John Bellhouse was waiting for it outside the house when I arrived.

"Had a good weekend?" he asked.

"Yes" I replied shiftily.

"Er - all in one piece then?" he asked. Funny question, I thought to myself.

My resolve cracked. "Well, I did put a couple of very small dents in the car but I had them straightened out."

At this he burst out into fits of laughter and fell on the ground rolling, kicking his legs in the air.

"Funny" I thought to myself.

It turned out that by a complete chance they had heard what had happened and had been killing themselves with laughter all day wondering what condition their new car was going to be in and what line I could possibly take to explain it away.

The Taunton matches themselves were perhaps unique in the whole history of sport in that we were awarded the cup for losing the first match. The game on the Saturday afternoon was for the Sheikh's Cup, one of a number distributed around English clubs after the Aden Polo Club was forced to suspend business due to the change of management in that corner of the Arabian peninsula. We lost the game and it was evident that the Taunton Club was rather put out that it was going to have to find storage space for the enormous silver pot for yet another year. The Taunton Club is famous for the scale of its hospitality to visiting teams and they laid on a splendid party at somebody's castle for us that night. Fortified by this, we managed to win our match against the Royal Navy the next day and as we crowded into the member's enclosure after the game to receive our prizes, we were amazed to see the same enormous silver pot, which we had competed for and lost the day before, being wheeled out with grim determination from the depths of the Club House as the trophy for this match too. They were determined to unload the thing onto us. Perhaps it was 'hot' property or the committee in session had decided they could no longer afford the insurance on such a cumbrous and exotic piece.

* * *

It was through Polo that I was to have two more brief encounters with the Royal Family during my last year. The Queen came down to Oxford to open something or other and as Visitor of Oriel College, a position held by the monarch since Edward II founded the establishment as Black Prince, she was due to make an inspection and have dinner in Hall. I had completely forgotten about this as the Varsity match was only two weeks away and we were concentrating hard on beating Cambridge. I had spent the afternoon playing polo at Kirtlington Park and bowled in through the main gates of Oriel to find quite a number of people hanging about the front quad, which was unusual. Somebody reminded me of the Queen's visit and at that moment the Royal Progress came in through the gates I had just gone through, the Queen at its head and Harold Macmillan, the Vice-Chancellor of the University, somewhere close behind. Now by 1968 well over half the undergraduates had succumbed to the current uniform of long and dirty hair set off by scruffy clothes and more or less revolutionary poses - a uniform adopted rather patronisingly by the 'progressive' offspring of the gin and jaguar belt from the comfort of their Esher homes and with less accuracy, less self-consciousness and more permanent conviction by the genuine sons of workers who actually spent more time working for their degrees and less time in the promotion of the revolution which the former group arrogantly presented as being in their best interest. The front quad appeared to be so full of these people that one could have been forgiven for thinking that the entire cast of the 'Beggar's Opera' in contemporary dress had been assembled for the opening night. I suppose that I must have stood out a mile with my Aldershot hairstyle, breeches and polo boots. Whatever it was, the Queen homed in on this more familiar pattern of dress and I was horrified to see her advance steadily on me across the quad. In that voice so familiar since my earliest years, from Christmas broadcasts and grants of Independence to dusky nations around the globe, barely able to restrain their incipient revolutions and counter revolutions even while the flags were being hauled down and run up in their several stadiums of the National Redeemer, she asked: "Are most of the people here in this college?"

Now I had never clapped eyes on any of the people there before in my life, but this was not the moment for contentious comments. With singular lack of originality and all the fluency of an expensive education, I heard myself saying:

"Yes, I think that, in fact, most of the people who are, in fact, here today, are, in fact, in this college."

The Queen appeared satisfied with the elaborate pearl of wisdom and then performed a manoeuvre which I was to witness again two weeks later. She made a slight movement backwards, simultaneously flashing a wide warm smile and an icy stare, a regal and silent equivalent of "time to come in number 32, your time is up!" which leaves the recipient in no doubt that that will be all, thank you.

* * *

Two weeks later, the Varsity Polo match took place. As usual, Lord Cowdray gave us the run of his stables for any horses we wanted, which was all the more important this year as the Prince of Wales had largely mounted the Cambridge side on ponies from Windsor. A large crowd had gathered at Kirtlington and there had been publicity for the event for some time previously. By tradition we shared the car park receipts for the Varsity match with the Kirtlington Club and finances therefore looked good for next year. Before lunch, we joined Prince Charles and the Cambridge team for drinks in brilliant sunshine on the terrace at Kirtlington Park, overlooking the former Italian garden with its sweeping view down to the lake. The Oxford team lunched with their captain Julian Eeley, at Northbrook farm where we kept the ponies that summer. Shortly before the start of the match the Queen arrived with Colonel Miller in a maroon 3.5 litre Rover and the Duke of Edinburgh drove his black drophead Alvis.

Prince Charles scored in the first chukka with a back-hander from a melée in front of the Oxford goal and it was not until the second chukka that we equalised after Julian split the Cambridge defense and passed up a ball that I could hardly fail to put through the Cambridge goal. By the end of the fourth chukka we were still drawn after a somewhat ragged but even game, with most of the Cambridge work being done by Prince Charles, The Umpires decided to widen the goal mouths and play a deciding chukka. Within 50 seconds Oxford had won. Luckily, I was riding Orchid, and playing number one, was able to hit the ball up the field at the throw in. Orchid gave it all she had as we shot away and with a couple more hits I took the ball up to the Cambridge goal where I lost it but Clive Preston came thundering through to put it firmly between the posts.

In the enclosure after the game, we were presented to the Queen who gave German alarm clocks to the winning team. This time we had a much longer and more fluent conversation without allusion to our previous encounter. When I got the 'Time to come in number 32' look again, it was simply so that the Queen could talk to the others in the team.

When the second game of the afternoon was over the Queen returned to Windsor Castle and we saw Prince Charles drive off in his blue MGC GT. We assumed that he had returned to Windsor too. We started to pack up after a few drinks in the bar and the rest of the team started to change. Julian took a telephone call in the clubhouse. He put the telephone down and asked me to get down to Northbrook farm as soon as I could. When I got there I found Prince Charles happily having tea but with very little company to talk to. It was about half an hour before the rest of the teams got out of the showers and made it down to the farm. We therefore had a long conversation together, ranging from the bullhorn he had recently fitted to his car and which apparently drove the cows into a frenzy at Sandringham, to some sallies into world affairs. I was left with the impression of a perceptive and lively mind and at the certain risk of sounding both patronising and sycophantic, it is worth recording that I felt that Britain would be fortunate in having such a man at the head of a society which is likely to witness much change in the future.

* * *

I have to admit that polo is a game which has an irresistible fascination for me. Like an alcoholic who has the choice of complete indulgence or strict teetotalism, polo is a game which I have to play with all my might and complete devotion, or leave completely alone. Once or twice since leaving Oxford I have played but with unsatisfactory results. My fitness was gone, or the ponies were not to my liking and I found that I had lost some of the instinct of being in the right place at the right time so that the games have left me dissatisfied.

I started playing polo in Libya, on an attachment to the 5th Royal Inniskilling Dragoon Guards in Benghazi, I was later to join the reserve of this noble regiment as a member of that select unit known as Stephenson's Horse. The ponies were mostly barbs straight off the hills or rescued from lives between shafts and the games were enlivened by the incorrigible mouths of the mounts. Whereas "having pony trouble" in the UK means a strained tendon or a minor vice requiring a few hours schooling, "pony trouble" in Libya meant that someone somewhere was being taken for a ride which had little to do with the game in hand. It was not uncommon while this was happening for the horse and rider to disappear behind one of the houses dotted around the mud pitch to rejoin the game several minutes later. Sometimes a game would go on around one of those enormous black Cadillacs with baroque bumpers driving straight across the ground with its complement of Sheikhs in flowing robes. One of King Idris' nephews, the Black Prince, lived in a palace beside the pitch and the story goes that one day a score of Senussi tribesmen galloped in from the desert firing off their rifles as they went, whether in joy or in anger, no one was very sure, riding straight across the pitch while a game was in progress. The barb ponies took off at this and eight very bewildered officers found themselves involuntarily carried towards the walls of the Prince's palace, while rifles went off with great elan and little regard for accuracy, all around them. Since then I have played in England, Germany and Cyprus. Although it is a sport which has acquired a very exclusive aura this is not really the case. All the Clubs are open to any who can afford it and service polo is open to all ranks. Outside the services, a certain amount of money is required, but no more than is required to run a motor car of more than 2.5 litres and considerably more is required to run a modest boat or yacht. It is such an exciting game both to play and to watch and can be so rewarding, that I am tempted to reflect that if all malcontents took it up there would be little trouble in the world.

* * *

Towards the end of my third year I was having lunch with Justin at the Grid. It was a fine hot day and the thought of working that afternoon appalled us both. Justin suggested we buy a bottle of claret and take a couple of the polo ponies out from Middleton for some exercise. We could find a field somewhere, tie up the horses, drink the wine and go to sleep in the sun. What a splendid idea! We went downstairs to the Peugeot and as we drove down Cornmarket passed a girl we knew and invited her to join us. She accepted and a little further on we saw John Slater and his girlfriend and they joined up too and added a second bottle to the party. We stopped briefly to pick up some boots at John's College where we ran into Salim, an engaging polo player from Pakistan, scarcely five feet tall but the possessor of a giant size capacity for amusement. He joined us enthusiastically but asked us to wait five minutes. We stood about impatiently, anxious to make the most of this glorious afternoon as soon as possible. After some minutes Salim suddenly burst into view, completely obscured, bar his legs and hands, by an enormous crate of a dozen bottles of champagne. Up went the boot of the Peugeot, in went the crate and we were off like a bat out of hell. We suspected there might be a connection between the Champagne and the stock laid in by the Committee for the college dance the previous night, but questions would have been indelicate and besides, a successful afternoon was now well within our grasp.

Salim had with him a beautiful French girl to whom he was extending some fairly permanent hospitality at the time. She was superlatively endowed, blonde and supposedly learning English at one of the language schools. Someone must have blown it, for not long afterwards Salim had to cope with an angry mother who had flown over from Paris to redeem her daughter from his den of oriental iniquities.

At the stables the three Australian girls and another couple completed the party and we soon had a dozen ponies saddled up. We rode out about two miles to a secluded avenue of trees between two minor roads where we tied a rope across the ride between trees and tied up the ponies on alternate sides, removing the saddles. We settled down and drank the wine, watching a few lazy insects and butterflies hovering over the long grass which bent in a slight breeze. When we finished the wine, we started on the champagne. The woods echoed to the sounds of popping corks and increasingly careless laughter as we passed the frothing bottles. We began to realise that we could never drink through the crate. We started dueling with unopened bottles, firing the corks at each other, much to the bewilderment of the ponies which had been watching the scene placidly with an occasional swish of the tail to drive off the flies. They began tugging at their ropes. Judgment was by now seriously impaired. I decided that my pony would like half a bottle of champagne and Justin filled his up with a half too. They drank eagerly, poor things.

Somebody was foolish enough to suggest a game of polo in a field nearby. Three a side, two people on each pony, no saddles. Instead of a ball we used a sweater, rather as the Afghans play using a dead calf or sheep. I drew the French girl and mounted behind her. She had, as I mentioned, a superb chest and there was really nothing else for me to hold onto. We galloped madly round the field after successive holders of the sweaters. Inevitably, I began to feel us slowly slipping out of the vertical. It was a matter of time before we fell off. The field had just been cut and there were straw bales piled up in various places, Marie-Louise steered towards the nearest pile and as we galloped past we fell off into the straw.

Sometime later, I remounted and thought it a fit moment to find out just how fast my new pony would go. Disaster. We shot off across the field. Without a saddle and in a weakened state I slipped off, unfortunately underneath the animal and its hooves caught me in most places, including the back of my head. The next thing I knew was a furious Suzy standing over me holding Orchid, who had bolted and had had a narrow brush with a gravel lorry on the road.

It was time to go. We walked the ponies back to the stables. I remember riding up next to Salim, who always rode the largest animal in the stables, Caburé. Caburé was clumsy and prone to swerving away from or towards the ball without any discernible pattern. If he didn't want to play polo that day he would put an enormous hoof on top of a ball in play and stamp it irretrievably into the ground. He was also a good jumper and could be hunted during the winter. But for all his quirks he could be relied on and now he knew what was required of him. He had to take his rider home. Salim was prostrate along Caburé's neck, an arm hanging limply down each side. I caught Salim by his shirt collar- and pulled him up right as I rode alongside. Two white eyes rolled towards me in a dusky face.

"Oh please, John, let me down!" he groaned, I dropped him back down on the horse's neck and Caburé took him home.

CHAPTER FOUR

LEGAL AND ANCIENT

Relations between undergraduates and the Police were good. The days when every self respecting undergraduate sported a policeman's helmet in his rooms had long since gone. The colleges could only be entered by the police on the invitation of the Dean, a hangover perhaps from the days when the University was subject only to Canon Law, but the police rarely did come into the colleges. Sometimes an undergraduate might have property stolen from his rooms, often by thieves plausibly dressed as undergraduate complete with gowns, in which case the police would investigate, but they preferred to leave minor disciplinary matters to College Deans and the Universities' own proctors. No doubt, the police took a discreet interest towards the end of the 1960's, when Oxford failed to escape entirely the spate of demonstrations, sit-ins and so on which afflicted most of the Universities of the world. Sometimes there would be scuffles when an outside speaker arrived, whose views did not coincide with those of one or other of the political factions in the University, and usually it was those groups which complained most bitterly about restriction of democracy and the right to protest, which attempted most violently to stifle the opinions of those with whom they disagreed.

The spirit of cooperation which existed between University and Police is well portrayed in the experience of a friend at Oriel after a good dinner at which he had not stinted on the wine. He managed to delude himself into believing that he was driving a motor car as he walked back up St Aldates towards Carfax in the middle of the road. Whenever an obstruction to his passage appeared he would meticulously change gear with his left hand, using the clutch with his left foot, all the while gripping an imaginary steering wheel with his right hand. There was always a policeman late at night at Carfax and his slow progress up the white line in the middle of the road was observed by the Officer on duty that night with some curiosity. Finally, as my friend arrived at Carfax the lights went red against him and he braked hard, put on the handbrake and stuck out his arm to indicate a right turn down the High Street. The Officer went across to him and asked him how far he intended to drive that night:

"As far as Oriel College" was the reply, at which the policeman took him gently by the arm and drove him home along the pavement.

Away from Oxford things could be rather different. I was driving out of London one night with Gavin Tweedie, a Household Cavalry Officer with whom I was sharing a cottage on the edge of Oxford at the time. We had both been at a dinner party and I was not too sure of the way onto the M4 motorway and made one false turn, which I soon corrected, failing to notice that this perfect legal manoeuvre had been observed by a police patrol car. As we drove towards the Chiswick roundabout the patrol car overtook, flashing its blue light and ordering us to stop. I pulled in and four policemen tumbled out of the car and surrounded us. One was in very scruffy plain clothes. They managed to give every appearance of a bunch of cowboys looking for some trouble to have a bit of fun with. They asked whether the car was mine, which clears them, since the police can stop any motor car on suspicion that it might be stolen. I asked why we had been stopped, and was told that I had taken a wrong turning and was driving on dipped headlights, which for some reason which I have never understood, used not to be the fashion in London. Now the breathalyser had just been brought in and cases of its use achieved wide prominence in the Press. It became quite clear after some time and a number of questions about where we had been and how much we had had to drink, that these cowboys were looking for an excuse to use their new toy. They went round the car looking for cracked reflectors, dirty number plates and loose bumpers, which might have given them the excuse they needed to bring out the breathalyser. They conferred amongst themselves and it was evident that they were unable to find a reasonable excuse. Throughout they had been thoroughly objectionable and finally one of them pointed to my extinguished lights (extinguished in response to his earlier request to turn everything off) and said:

"That wasn't very sensible, was it?"

To which I replied:

"When I want to be taught common sense by you I will ask, thank you very much."

To which he replied:

"Quite often your type needs to be taught common sense."

At this juncture Gavin asked:

"And just what exactly is my type?"

And the response came forth:

"If you don't know by now, God help you!"

Promising stuff. We took their numbers, which they told us at the time failed to impress them, they got back into their car and we drove back to Oxford.

We both made complaints to the Commissioner of the Metropolitan Police over the incident since apart from their very objectionable manner, our detention had been tantamount to a random breath test, something which the Home Secretary had assured the House the previous week would not be permitted.

Now any complaint made against the Police has to be investigated and a very charming and diplomatic Chief Inspector was sent from the local police station in Oxford to take a statement from me. We discussed the incident, which he agreed was most regrettable and I said that as far as I was concerned the point had been made and I was prepared to drop the matter. The Chief Inspector beamed and thanked me for understanding so well the difficulties of the Police Force and as he left the house he asked, in all seriousness:

"By the way, are you interested in joining the Police? We need men like you!"

Gavin's experience was not much different. Our cottage fell into a different administration area for the Police and early one morning the local Chief Inspector rang up to ask if he could come and see him. I said that later that evening Gavin would be in and this seemed to suit the Chief Inspector very well. "About quarter to eleven tonight then?" he suggested. As it happened both of us knew this gentleman for completely different reasons. It vaguely coursed through my brain that 10.45 p.m. was just after the pubs closed in Oxford in those days and sure enough, when the Chief Inspector drove across the farmyard slightly erratically, got out of his car and weaved uncertainly towards the door, I felt justified in confirming my suspicions. We brought out a bottle of whisky and had a rare old yarn together until midnight.

At one stage I was the brief owner of a very highly tuned TR 3 sports car which combined a top speed of 110 m.p.h. with a minimum of roadholding. While driving back over Salisbury Plain one Sunday with a girl, the entire exhaust system disintegrated and fell off. The result was a fiendish roar from the unsilenced engine. We went out for dinner and my companion missed her last train back to London so that I had to take her down to Reading where there was a later train. As I turned into Holywell Street after dinner with a good load of alcohol in my system, I found that by revving the engine in the narrow street I could make a tremendous racket which echoed off the tall houses on either side. I was happily amusing myself at this game down the street, when to my horror, I saw a figure in dark blue step off the pavement into the road and hold up a hand to stop me. I stood no chance of passing a breath test and I knew that I had committed a clear offence this time.

"Good evening Sir" came the deep, measured tones of a stage bobby.

"Good evening Officer"

"This car is making a lot of noise isn't it"

"Yes Officer, I am afraid the exhaust fell off today, and being Sunday, I haven't been able to get it repaired"

"I see Sir, and have you got far to go tonight?"

"Well, I'm afraid that I have to take the young lady down to Reading to catch a train"

"I see Sir. Very well, proceed upon your way, bearing in mind the time of night and the fact that people are at home abed trying to get some sleep!"

"Good night Sir!"

* * *

My favourite brush with the Law, however, came one summer evening after a visit to watch the Cowdray Gold Cup played at Cowdray Park. It had been a thrilling game played in bright sunshine on the beautiful Abbey Ground, against a continuous buzz of the millionaire's helicopters delivering players, or whisking them back to their city offices or country houses. A group of us stopped for dinner on the way back at the Red Lion Hotel in Basingstoke High Street. Once again we dined and wined without moderation and I turned into the High Street from the Red Lion with Murdoch Laing, a colourful Canadian, Justin Cartwright from South Africa and Bertie Boyd from Northern Ireland in the car. It was only when I saw this police car coming towards me with its light flashing, the driver with mouth open in amazement and a hand out of the window signaling me to stop, that I realised that I was driving the wrong way down a one way street. I kept going straight on, professing not to notice the police car and doing my best to ignore the drunken glee of my passengers, exhorting me to put my foot down and high tail it out of Basingstoke at top speed. I resisted this invitation to provide an after dinner cabaret, but took a very devious route out to the by-pass, where to my astonishment the police car found us and signaled to stop. I knew once again that there was no hope of passing a breathalyser test and resolved to brazen it out in the spirit of a horrified innocent. This clearly required all the stops pulled out and I got out of the car as steadily as possible and in my most earnestly puzzled tone said:

"Good evening, Officer, now what seems to be the trouble?"

"Good evening Sir, were you aware that you were driving the wrong way down a one way street?"

"Good heavens, no, Officer"

Justin and Murdoch were in the meantime up to mischief behind me. I tried not to notice what was going on as they got out of the car and started fighting with each other on the verge like overgrown schoolboys. After a bit they tired of this and walked out into the roadway trying to stop cars and signal them into the side so that they too might benefit from an interview with the policeman. The policeman was watching these antics over my shoulder and for the second time that evening I saw that same look of amazement in his eyes as the game developed in the road way. I went on:

"I am afraid I have never been to Basingstoke before in my life, Officer, and I didn't realise that it was a one way street."

By now the situation behind me was getting out of hand and the policeman obviously thought it best to bring the whole business to the speediest conclusion possible:

"If you can get those two apes off the road and back into your car, I will say Good night Sir!"

"Good night Officer."

He sprinted for his car and drove away in evident relief.

* * *

The University had its own police force in the form of the Proctors, two dons elected for two years to deal with disciplinary matters relating to undergraduates and a staff of half a dozen "Bulldogs" led by the University Marshall. Originally the powers of this little band must have been quite considerable as they had formerly been the executors of the Canon Law to which the University used to be subject. Up to the beginning of the nineteenth century they theoretically had the right to hang undergraduates from Magdalen Bridge. Up to the First World War one of their more colourful tasks was to round up all the tarts who came town from London on the evening train, put them in the cells in the Clarendon Building overnight if they managed to catch them, and send them back to Shepherds Market on the milk train in the morning.

The Proctors, in my day, used to codify the less obscure rules of the University in a booklet which appeared annually, called the Proctor's Memorandum. This governed all sorts of things from restrictions on keeping aircraft in the vicinity of Oxford to regulations governing behaviour "liable to bring the name of the University into disrepute" (a pretty wide one, that). They were also responsible for ensuring that sub-fusc, a uniform of dark suit, black shoes and sock, white shirt, white bow tie, scholars or commoner's gown and cap (or mortar board) was worn for examinations, matriculation, degree ceremonies, appearances in court etc. One of their quainter habits was to patrol the streets of Oxford at night from time to time. This patrol consisted of the

University Marshall in front, the two proctors in full academic dress, white bow ties, and six or so "bulldogs" in bowler hats bringing up the rear in military ranks of two. Originally, the proctor's patrol broke up riotous brawls between town and gown and, before the Second War, ensured that undergraduates did not frequent public houses. Now their role was more or less prophylactic, but the bulldogs were still picked for their fleetness of foot in a chase.

The stories of those who dug up old and obsolete rules were legion. Perhaps the best known is that of the examination candidate who called, according to ancient custom, for beer and sandwiches during his exam. These were provided, but shortly thereafter he found himself summoned to appear before the proctors, who quoted another obsolete rule and fined the undergraduate for not wearing a sword with his sub-fusc.

Looking through old statutes could be profitable. Once we thought we were onto a good thing when we discovered that in the Seventeenth century the Earl of Clarendon left £100,000 to the University for the pursuit of equestrian sports by undergraduates. This sum must have compounded into millions of pounds over the years and we thought that a slice of it would improve the quality of the Draghounds and our polo ponies no end. As it happened, we were only about forty years too late, since the money was eventually spent by the University on building the Clarendon laboratories.

In my first year, I was summoned to appear before the proctors endless times on account of my motor car, which one was at that time forbidden to keep or park in Oxford until one had passed the Preliminary examination and obtained the consent of one's College. (When one did obtain permission for a motor car, it had to carry a small green light on the front to mark it out as an undergraduate's car. Apparently this was not legal and an Oxford man was once fined by a Cambridge court for this. His defense was not accepted.)

This hardly made sense since I lived in Oxford anyway and could legally run one during the vacations. Nevertheless I lost count of the number of times I was fined two pounds. Once, after payment, the proctor asked: "Now, what is all this about you knocking the University Marshall off his moped?" I was genuinely nonplussed, and then dimly recalled a character a week previously in a grubby canvas mackintosh, gauntlets and bicycle-clips hammering on the hood of my car and complaining that I had forced him into the side at the traffic lights beside the Clarendon building. I offered the incident as the one the proctor might be referring to, adding that it was a ludicrous charge and whoever it was doing the hammering on my roof clearly had a grudge against young men with motor cars while he only had a moped. The proctor replied "I quite agree. Case dismissed."

I finally became very bored with my continual appearances before the proctors and when they raised my fines from two to three pounds, I declared that a fine could only be interpreted as a licence to commit an offence and not as a deterrent or punishment, unless an alternative of imprisonment was offered. Next time I would opt for imprisonment in the cells below, formerly frequented by those ladies of easy virtue. I suspected that this would be a new one for the proctors and that the problems of feeding, exercising, and guarding a prisoner would be too much for them. The proctor to whom I made this statement was visibly astonished and commented that he would seek legal advice on this point. It must have been good advice since I was never again summoned to appear before the proctors.

I got my own back anyway. One summer Corpus Christi College, next door, became Head of the River and had the customary celebratory dinner. Unfortunately this one got badly out of control and there was considerable rowdyism inside the college. At one stage the fire brigade was called to put out a small fire and one of the Corpus men hi-jacked the fire engine and drove it away. Regrettably one of the firemen was badly hurt in the melee, something which was quite rightly taken very seriously afterwards. Word soon got around that things were pretty riotous around Corpus and the proctors hastily called out their patrol to quieten things down in the streets near the college. Everyone in Oriel was ready to take full advantage of the situation as the chances of a good scrap when Corpus came out of dinner were very good indeed. When the proctors and the police arrived we had to retreat into Oriel, where about two dozen of us manned the walls above the kitchens in Magpie Lane. Every twenty minutes or so the proctors' patrol would pass up the lane and we hurriedly assembled buckets of water and various missiles to pour down on them. I happily remember scoring several direct hits with the water on the proctors and bulldogs who were scrutinising their attackers for old faces. One of the proctors suffered a severe blow to his head and dignity when I caught him fair and square on his cap with a lavatory roll. How sweet was revenge! They attempted several times to enter Oriel College to deal with us, but like the police they had to have the Dean's permission and the latter remained firmly unavailable!

CHAPTER FIVE

BALLS

Every year each College would hold a ball, towards the end of the summer term. Every three years a college would hold a Commemoration Ball, which in practical terms meant that the occasion was rather more dignified, on a large scale and one could expect a greater number of the fellows to attend, since the "Commems" had the official backing of the Senior Common Room. All these balls were ambitious projects and occasionally two Colleges might combine. There were usually two bands, playing in different parts of the college and a discotheque. Marquees were often erected in the quads or gardens of the Colleges to accommodate dancers, or for dining. Some of the rooms would be designated for "sitting out". At the larger functions there might be as many as six bands playing simultaneously, together with numerous amusements such as fortune tellers, shooting booths, dodgem cars and fairground machines and there would always be a 'big-name' entertainer. This was usually in the form of a top pop group who, while I was at Oxford, charged more and more exorbitant fees for less and less playing time, until by the time I left £2000 for three-quarters of an hour was quite usual. After this brief performance they would drive off to another engagement that night somewhere else. Most of these groups were on drugs during their appearances and the standard of their play could vary enormously. Sometimes you were lucky if they were conscious enough to face their audience rather than the back of the marquee. Nevertheless, it was a weird experience to see these creatures of the night, beings from a different world, enact their frantic music and purge their several trances in the hall built by the Black Prince or the quad left half finished by Cardinal Wolsey when he fell from Grace.

However foreign and worldly such alien intrusions might be, and however urgently this message from a different culture might be put across by powerful amplifiers, the dignified atmosphere of the colleges was an inescapable background and their yellow Headington and Bath stone observed and cast judgement with the authority of centuries. For pop music is a culture of channeled frustration and rebellion which the colleges have doubtless seen ebb and flow over the centuries in the spirit of the youth in their care. This manifestation might be less harmful than the medieval riots between town and gown, than the profligacy of the eighteenth century, or the hearty jingoism of the nineteenth, but on all might be cast the judgement of transient phenomena. One had only to stroll into the maturity of a fine college garden in the twilight of a summer evening while the urgent brouhaha reverberated within, to realise which of the two cultures was tolerating which, with benign, but patronising confidence.

Tickets for these balls were expensive, largely on account of the cost of hiring well known groups or dodgem cars and if one had no particular regard for the girl, or else knew her well enough for it not to matter, the option for the impecunious and the adventurous was to gatecrash. Elaborate precautions were taken to prevent this, such as the erections of thick coils of barbed wire in all the likely places, or the hiring of private security organisations to patrol the ground with dogs. Equally elaborate devices were used to gain illicit entry to the point of forging tickets, although this was frowned on. The colleges were, of course, built three of four centuries ago when buildings were designed with security in mind. Walls were purposely built with few windows at ground level, and those that there were had bars. There were few places where one could climb in, and these were well known since in those days college gates were locked around midnight and afterwards one had to climb in by one of these routes. Each college generally had one easy means of entry known only to the undergraduates, but when there were balls, this was always heavily fortified with barbed wire. The chink in the armour was the main gate, through which the guests entered and the greatest number of successful 'crashings' was effected here. It was a question of superiority of wits and the college porters knew most of the tricks. The standbys were to pretend to be a member of the band or, if you didn't feel like putting on a dinner jacket, to be a hanger on of one of the Pop groups, such as "Roadie", manager or driver. Justin Cartwright wrote himself a letter purporting to come from the bandleader at Brasenose ball giving him instructions on how to get to the college. He then turned up with an instrument case, showed the porter the letter and asked where to find the rest of the band. He was directed without further question. It was always more difficult if there was a girl, as they were not so good at climbing and it was less easy to get them through the gate with a plausible story. One of the best successes while I was at Oxford, was in fact a couple who turned up immaculately dressed and then had a convincing argument in the main gateway. Finally the girl burst into tears, and before the astonished crowd, slapped her partner hard in the face before dashing into the college. Her partner rushed after her to heal the rift and nobody lifted a finger to stop them.

* * *

I only crashed two balls at Oxford and I never really approved of the habit which some people made of it. It always seemed so very unfair on those who paid a lot of money to get in. It irritated me intensely to see obvious crashers at a ball for which I had paid a lot of money for tickets. I once crashed a ball at Pembroke college with a girl whom I knew only moderately well. We walked twice round the outside of the college without spotting a way in. It is a notoriously difficult college to get into at the best of times. The most obvious place had floodlights trained on it, a good deal of barbed wire and two guards. We were about to give up when, incredibly, a door opened in a high wall beside Brewer Street and three people walked out. We dashed in before the door shut and found ourselves in the Fellow's garden. We heard someone coming and I pushed the girl onto a seat, flung myself upon her and silenced her astonishment with a long kiss. Whoever it was shone a torch at us but did not interrupt the touching scene to ask why we were there. He did, however, lock the door behind him and left us trapped in the garden. I had to force a window with a metal comb into the master's lodgings, where we found ourselves in a bedroom next to a room in which elderly voices could be heard talking. We crept out into a corridor and let ourselves out into the main part of the college. After that ball was over, I had considerable trouble getting back into my own college in the early morning. Our climbing in route had been blocked by the management when Charles Townshend left a ladder up against it. This upset both the Dean and the branch of Barclays Bank the other side of Magpie Lane, which felt that leaving ladders about compromised its security. Charles said afterwards that he could remember neither leaving the ladder there, nor indeed climbing in at all, or anything after his last drink, but the damage was done. Henceforth we had to climb up a sheer wall with few foot or hand holds. This was quite difficult, especially if you had been to a good party or were smartly dressed. Eventually someone fell and hurt their back quite badly trying to climb in and quite a lot of pressure was brought on the colleges to give undergraduates keys if they wanted to come in late. Most colleges did this a year or so after I went down. Usually I would park my car alongside the wall, climb on the roof and then jump for the top of the wall, which made it quite easy. This time

I was without my car and I did not fancy tearing my very ancient and already fragmentary dinner jacket in the climb. I was standing in Magpie Lane wondering what to do at about 5:30 a.m. when I heard the rattle of milk crates. Sure enough a milk cart turned the corner from Merton Street and before I even asked the driver for a favour he shouted:

"Usual place, then, guvnor?"

"Please" I said, and he positioned the cart exactly where I used to park my car. He gave me a hand up onto a crate of gold tops and wished me good-day.

The second time I crashed a ball it was a rather different story. I was sitting in the garden at Justin's digs in one of those houses which are unique to North Oxford. Enormous, well built Victorian family houses, the gardens, generous by the standards of today, full of mature trees, the interiors unchanged for fifty years. Nowadays, inhabited by the remaining daughters and widows of men who had served the Empire well, the high-ceilinged rooms are museums of a life which has vanished. Indian carpets cover the centre of the rooms leaving an eighteen inch gap of stained and polished floorboards as a frame. Oriental antiques, the legacy of oriental childhoods, furnish these chambers of the past with a profusion which would be the envy of serious collectors. Their owners, with all the manners and standards of a bygone era, have never seen them with collector's eyes. The number, alas, sadly dwindles year by year. At least one of the inhabitants of this particular house, a Tibetan monk, who periodically shouted for quiet into the garden below, must have felt strangely at home in this compromise of time and place.

As we sat round a table crowded with chicken paella and rosé d'Anjou in the long summer evening, we discussed the security measures being taken for the Magdalen Commem that night. Securicor had been hired along with several guard dogs, a lot of wire had been put up and the tickets carried an ultra violet code to prevent forgery. The organisers guaranteed those who paid £12 for tickets that it was a crash-proof ball. With a challenge like that it was hardly surprising at that time that Justin, myself and Alan Gordon-Walker, whose father was at that time a prominent member of the Labour Cabinet, decided to have a go. We decided that an entirely new story would have to be fabricated to get through the gate as a forced entry seemed unlikely to achieve much success in view of the elaborate guard system. We happened to run into one of the caterers who said that if we could get in, he would provide us with food and drink. It seemed worth a try. The three of us went first of all to a very good Italian restaurant nearby whose proprietor was well known to us. From him we acquired three authentic chef's outfits and a number of the tools of the trade, such as carving knives and forks, which we put ostentatiously on top of our folded dinner jackets in a grubby airline bag. We had all we needed. We drove down to Magdalen in a minivan and as we went down Longwall Street we saw would be crashers being prised off lamp posts by the Securicor guards on top of the walls. It looked as if our basic premise was correct. After parking the van we approached the gate on foot and saw a large crowd of ejected crashers on the pavement opposite discussing tactics. We encountered one who had been thrown out who said that he had just been chased and caught by a large Alsatian. We strode into the gate.

"Snooks caterers, come to carve the kedgeree for breakfast!"

Or some such opening gambit. For a moment we thought it had worked. Then the porter said yes, they were expecting Snooks caterers but did not believe we were them for a moment. We tried to bluff it out, but to no avail. Before we knew what was happening, a press photographer appeared from nowhere and sealed our fate:

"Hold it! Hold it! I want to get a photograph of some real crashers!" Click, flash, and that was it. Mug-shots for prosperity.

We still thought it was worth trying the same tactics again straight away at the back entrance, only this time we would drive in. We drove round to the gates at the rear through which the food and drink was delivered and found two Securicor guards, on this gate. We gave them the same story and one went off to check it with our caterer friend. The second guard proceeded to fill us in, with fascinating detail, on why he worked for security firms every summer. Money and girls mainly. We thought it was going to work when the second guard returned saying that the caterer wasn't expecting anymore staff that night. We felt badly down. The guards congratulated us on a good try and bade us good night.

CHAPTER SIX

OF WORK

At the end of my second summer term my tutor suggested that it would be germane for me to actually witness some of the French classical plays which I wrote about in my essays every week with a minimum of factual acquaintance. And so it was that late in September I drove over for two weeks to see as much French theatre as was possible in the time before term started again. As it happened I was to see two plays a day almost every day for a fortnight, usually one at the Comédie Française and one elsewhere. The strict classicism of the Comédie Française remains in my memory, but the productions were nevertheless imaginative and the cast always gave the impression of thoroughly enjoying the plays. The repertoire stretched to about two weeks. I remember also a performance of Cyrano de Bergerac whose capacity matinee audience consisted entirely of weeping women. At the other end of the scale I remember a quite superb performance by Jean-Louis Barrault in the "Tentation de St Antoine" at the Odéon.

The battered but speedy Peugeot 403 bowled down the autoroute to Paris at a steady 90 m.p.h. I arrived on the outskirts of the city and drove straight in to the Rue St Jacques on the left Bank. There I stopped the nearest American with a copy of "Europe on $5 a day" and flicked through it until I found the section on cheap hotels in the neighbourhood. I chose the Hotel Olinda on the Ile St Louis, 9 Francs a night, in those days about twelve shillings and sixpence. My room was up about six flights of stairs under the roof. I returned to this room my first night after a meal in the Latin Quarter. I hadn't realised just how thin the walls were, I think they must have been about one eighth of an inch of compressed hard-board papered over. There was the most incredible noise coming from the next room and at first I thought they were moving all the furniture round and rearranging it. The row was unbelievable, a hideous symphony of crashings and shudderings and bangings. By the time I had got into bed on my side of the thin partition I had guessed the true nature of the din. I was the privileged audience of a very accomplished performance. Finally, after more crashings, an exhausted French voice gasped out: "J'arrive! J'arrive!" And there was utter silence. I felt there was only one thing left for me to do. I sat up in bed and clapped politely.

***

Three months later I was back in France. Every year the Oxford, Cambridge and Trinity College Dublin Ski Clubs organised a joint skiing party abroad. Usually they went to Zürs in Austria, but prices there had been rising and it was felt that this year, as a matter of principle, the party should go elsewhere. Because the only possible time of the trip was December the choice was limited and Courchevel was picked on for 1967. I don't think Courchevel really knew what it was letting itself in for. Over the years Zürs had learnt to live with its troublesome client who by the way of compensation arrived at a low point in the season. Wives and daughters were sent to hiding places down the valleys, days before the first of the two or three hundred undergraduates arrived and extra supplies of liquor, including crates of Guinness for the Irishmen, were laid in specially. Anything fragile was boarded up and prayers were said. Courchevel was new to all this. At the best of times it exuded an aura of the worst French snobbism, and prided itself on being a veritable 'Paris dans la neige' basking in an air of exclusivity founded on very high prices. A root cause of early trouble was that in order to get the party at all, the hotels had had to put in very low bids, which they achieved by economising on food. This was a cardinal error, since the British and Irish were not prepared to make up for the lack of meat with bread and wine as Frenchmen might have done. It is only fair to say that the hotels varied very much in the deal that they gave, but some clearly felt that an address in Courchevel gave them the right to extract a great deal of money for very little service. It was nevertheless a good holiday, the weather was fine and the snow was quite adequate. It was snowing hard in Oxford when I left and a group of us in two cars had a pretty scary drive through the night with thick fog from Calais to Arras and a good deal of ice from Bourg-en-Bresse to Courchevel. Most of the two hundred skiers had travelled by a special train laid on by Justin Cartwright, the organizer of the whole holiday. Unfortunately for him, Britain devalued just as he was about to pay for the hire of this train and having exchanged a large number of Swiss Francs for Sterling, he was rumoured to have lost some thousands of pounds on the deal.

Several of us were sitting round after a particularly good fondue in our hotel one night wondering to do next. We were idly watching a succession of girls clothes which floated down past the window into a bank of snow outside as the ski team from a British cavalry regiment, also staying in the hotel, put in a little after hours training with an undergraduette. Our thoughts were thus drawn outside and Bertie Boyd announced that the previous night he had tried out his Triumph Spitfire on a gentle slope and found that, being very light it slid over the snow very well. It was all we needed. Eight of us crammed into the Peugeot in a bid to emulate this feat. There was a road which wound quite a long way up the mountain to some chalets beside the main piste. We set off up this road and found a place, where with very little spadework, we could drive off onto the ski slope. There was a drop of about five feet, but the Peugeot took it well without bogging its nose in the snow and we found ourselves on the piste with about a mile of steep slope ahead of us. We gathered speed until we were doing between thirty and forty miles an hour. To our amazement the car took it easily. It was an extraordinary experience drifting downhill round boulders and pine trees sideways at thirty miles an hour. The only difficult place was a narrow gap in a belt of pine trees followed by a short jump and I wondered whether the springs would take it. There was however no choice and I slewed the car from side to side to position it for the gap in the trees and we shot through. Immediately came the hummock in the snow and then we were briefly airborne. We made a perfect landing in the soft snow and continued across the nursery slopes to the car park and onto the road at the bottom. Our first trip in a skiing motor car had been an exhilarating experience and we set off to do a second and faster run now the technique of motorised parallel turns had been mastered.

I was awakened shortly before eight the next morning by a breathless Justin crashing into my room shouting "Get up John, you've got ten minutes to get out of town, the Police are after you!" I vaguely remembered the events of the previous night, but asked him why. "A lot of damage was done in the village last night and your car was seen about at the time." I groaned and rolled over in bed to pull the curtain aside. To my horror, I saw six gendarmes in line abreast walking up the road to the hotel. By the time I had slipped some clothes on they had surrounded the car and were taking notes. To my surprise they didn't come into the hotel and I found out later what the trouble had been. There were parallel lines of flagpoles along the road by the car park at the entrance to the upper part of the village. The Irish had climbed one of these to remove the French flag soon after our escapade with the Peugeot, and when the climber got to the top the aluminium pole slowly bent right across the road leaving the climber bouncing gently inches above the tarmac. This raised great possibilities. Within minutes all the poles had been climbed and bent in similar fashion across the road so that the road to the upper village was completely barred. To add insult to injury the only flags they removed were the Tricolors and the flags of European Unity. This exploit cost the Irish several hundred pounds to put right. I think Courchevel was quite glad to see the back of us.

* * *

Disaster struck. Whether it was the effect of the altitude at Courchevel, or the exhaustion of the long drives there and back, or whether it was simply a case of doing too much, or too little food and rest, I do not know, but early in January I began to realise that I was not well. In February I found that if I sat down for a moment in the JCR I fell asleep almost immediately and would wake up to find several hours had passed. Finally, I went to the college doctor who took a blood sample and shortly thereafter confirmed glandular fever, adding that it was one of the worst cases the Radcliffe Infirmary had ever seen. This was acutely serious, since I had only six months to go before my final exams. Up till now things had been going along quite well but now the prospect of a disastrous end to my Oxford career loomed ahead. Glandular fever is a wicked disease, but because it is not fatal, or thought very important, little research has been done on it. In a bad case the effects are devastating. One is prone to days of complete debilitation, unable to make any mental effort. Then quite suddenly the mind functions at great intensity and the body feels full of energy. The sufferer will then exhaust himself by a spurt of activity which the weakened body cannot support and the cycle then recommences with another period of worse debilitation. And so it goes on. It is a wicked disease because it makes almost any mental work very difficult and it strikes young people, usually students, at a time when they most need to make use of their brains. It is a wicked disease too because the sufferer so easily fools himself into thinking he is recovered during the cycles of high activity. I had had the disease eight years previously but in milder form. Then it lasted about two months. This time the effects were to last for two years.

I asked the doctor what could be done.

"Nothing" was the reply. He went on "Whatever amount of work you are doing each day, you must cut by half."

"You must be joking" I said, "I can only manage an hour and a half."

"Then, you must cut it down to three quarters of an hour, it is important not to strain yourself."

I tried a different tack. "Look" I said, "I find I can make physical effort with a bit of determination. I have just started to bring in the polo ponies to get them fit for the summer. I feel a bit of a fraud riding half the day and putting in so little work."

The answer was firm. "You can't hope to get strong and well again without getting some exercise. Carry on with the horses but cut your work down to three quarters of an hour a day."

And so it was. I went to my tutor who accepted the college doctor's decision without question. I suppose he had seen it all before. As the most acute stage passed I was able to do a little more work but the finals were too close for the effect not to show.

Apart from the time when the stables girls walked out, I had never failed to produce work during my three years at Oxford. It is true that I found some of the language translation classes superfluous but these were in any case optional extras. It is also true that after the preliminary examinations I dropped my second language, German, altogether. This was because I had learnt the language very quickly after changing subjects in midstream at school and my grammar, when written, left something to be desired. As a spoken language, it was more fluent than my French when I arrived at Oxford. For other reasons I now consider myself bilingual in French. My tutors (Christchurch) did not rate my German highly though, indeed one tutor told me to bring the first draft of my translation into German out of the Preliminary examination so that he could show me where I had failed. I was glad to be able to prove him wrong. In fact, taking both languages together I put up a better performance in Prelims than all the other linguists in my college, with the exception of one of the three scholars. However, I did opt for French alone for my finals. This had the advantage of marginally less work than coping with two languages, but this meant, on the other hand, a much deeper grasp of both language and literature as well as a greater number of papers in the final examination. One was, quite literally, expected to know everything about the development of French from Vulgar Latin. I went along with it quite happily, but there was a great deal of nitpicking in the philology which I always considered pretty phony. The basic theories were acceptable, but too many scholars had wasted too much postgraduate time trying to refine these theories with very little factual evidence to support them, so that much philology came to rest on the authority of a few subjective works of this and the preceding century, and in my view the subject had long since taken the step from science to faith. Besides, I just didn't like it!

I did, on the other hand, go to more lectures than most of my contemporaries. Indeed, it was amazing, when the final examinations came and everyone doing the same subject sat down in the same room, how many absolutely new faces there were which one had never seen at any lectures. I had, as well, two disadvantages. The first was a very concise and abrupt style. I noticed that when my contemporaries read their essays they would bang on for hours, explaining every detail and to my mind sometimes substituted length for perception and original thought. On the other hand I would see perhaps half a dozen points in a subject and list them straight away. The reaction was always the same. "Fine, but what about such and such, you only mentioned it briefly." I suppose examiners like to have it spelt out very slowly, but I always assumed a great deal and took acceptance and understanding of basic concepts for granted. The other disadvantage I can make no apology for. My handwriting is appalling. I even have trouble reading it myself.

I have always had two basic premises. First that I work better when under pressure and second, that with a modicum of organisation, it is possible to fit almost any amount of activities into twenty-four hours. On principle I never worked after 11 p.m. and out of preference I go to bed an hour earlier than that. I also think that recreation, both mental and physical, is essential if a man is to produce of his best in his daily work. It is so much a matter for regret that few institutions in later life recognise this, or provide their staff with the necessary facilities.

I have no argument with the examination system and find no fault with any system of gradings. Any fault here usually lies with the conclusions which unfamiliar minds draw from them. It may be that some day better systems will be devised but until then I am content with my lot. At the end of my last summer term it was, of course, necessary to sit the final examinations, a total of thirteen written papers and an oral examination in which to display the product of three years study. The written papers were unremarkable but the oral examination sticks in my mind.

Soon after I went in I realised that it had been a mistake to attend faithfully one very boring series of lectures. These were given by a pedantic and pasty faced man who no doubt was an expert in his subject, but certainly did not possess the gift of bringing it alive. He dealt mainly with the interpretation of manuscripts written by nearly anonymous monks in caves round the Mediterranean in the third and fourth centuries. These manuscripts showed clear intermediary stages between classical and vulgar Latin, which three years study at Oxford will convince you have an immeasurable bearing on the vocabulary of your Parisian taxi driver if you attempt to economise on his tip.

I had attended this man's turgid lectures faithfully and after the first one or two each term, attendance dropped to about ten, so he got to know the faces. I suppose I must have looked very disinterested, or spent too much time attempting to rival the lecturer for the attention of one or two of the girls who turned up, because he got his knife into me almost at once. In fact it became so obvious that the other examiner had to give him the equivalent of a referees warning once or twice. His first question was:

"Now, Mr Moir, this essay you have written on fourteenth century trends in French literature - you do realise that most of what you have written concerns the thirteenth and fifteenth centuries?"

I managed to parry that one moderately on the lines of origins and consequences, but the next one had me cold.

"Now, Mr Moir, this quotation from Dante's Canto V: "Il Lancelotto fu il libro", I seem to remember that when I read it it was "Il Libro fu il Lancelotto" what do you say to that?"

There was relatively little that I could say since the first time I came across the quotation was at dinner the night before the paper.

I realised too late during the viva that they were giving me the chance to improve the class of my degree and I am afraid that I did not rise to the occasion. When the results finally went up on the board, I looked first for my name among the second class Honours and was indignant not to find it there. I next looked at the fourth class Honours and the Pass Degrees and thankfully it was not there either. "Give yourself a break lad, and look at the first class!" It wasn't there either. It was a third, which is thought of as rather indeterminate. A good second or a first are respectable for obvious reasons and so is a fourth, as clear evidence that the recipient's energies were devoted elsewhere. But a third - difficult to put any sort of convincing label on it. I would say that I have only two regrets concerning my years at Oxford - one is the poor class of my degree, as I always expected to get a second, and the other, especially in view of the former, was my decision not to accept the Mastership of the University Draghounds.

I have one other regret and that has something to do with the English system of education, which forces such early specialisation on children. I specialised from the age of thirteen in science, which was a wrong move since I was devastatingly hopeless at all maths except trigonometry and geometry at which I shone very brightly; so I changed to languages, although I did best at English, and nobody told me the full range of courses at Oxford, or the fact that even if I got in on languages, there was nothing to stop me changing later. If I had known I would have done Arabic or Chinese or forestry or anything that had a greater rarity value and consequently better employment prospects. But schools don't think of such things and persist in teaching extinct tongues instead of law or accountancy which might be of direct use to their pupils in later life.

The ultimate comment on my academic career came some months later when I took part in one of those elaborate Latin ceremonies in the Sheldonian Theatre in order to receive my degree. All went with customary solemnity and ritual. The names were called and the owners went forward to receive the Latin accolade. All passed without incident until my name was read out as the recipient of an Honours degree. Somebody promptly threw a fit in the gallery.

CHAPTER SEVEN

GONE FOR A SOLDIER

Some weeks before the start of my first term at Oxford I joined one of the eight oldest units in the British Army and the last of these to exercise its privilege of carrying a halberd on parade.

The Oxford University Officers Training Corps, descended from a royalist body of the Civil War, had a small regular staff including a Colonel, Adjutant and Administrative Officer, together with up to a dozen regular N.C.O's. It was a little army in miniature with Infantry, Armour, Artillery, Signals, Engineers and Intelligence Sub-units. One joined as an Officer Cadet and if one passed a number of military examinations and tests one would hope to obtain a Regular or Territorial Army Commission. The strength of the Sub-units varied, and of course this was a period of extreme anti-military feeling in the country. Our own Armed Forces were being withdrawn from many parts of the world to be cut down and the Vietnam war was lending an aura of disrepute to any military activities in the minds of many people.

The Royal Armoured Corps sub-unit, successor to the old Cavalry Squadron, was always above strength, however, and there was competition to get in. Perhaps this was because it had the most glamorous role and equipment, among which were six Ferret scout cars. In my case, being a cavalryman at heart, it was this curious sub-unit of the Territorial Army which I joined in mid—September after swearing an oath of loyalty to the Queen on a very battered bible in the Adjutant's office. The O.T.C offered immense opportunities, since with so many sub-units it was possible to do all sorts of courses and go on attachments with the regular army overseas. I think many undergraduates had misconceptions about the T.A through their experiences in unimaginative Cadet Forces at school. Acknowledging that I put a lot into the O.T.C, I derived an enormous amount of benefit and satisfaction in return. At full strength the Armoured Corps sub-unit formed a complete armoured reconnaissance squadron and it was a most refreshing change from the nebulous problems of academic work to face the more immediate and concrete problems of commanding first a troop and then the squadron on exercises. These took places at weekends, either in the countryside around Oxford or on Salisbury

Plain, where we would sometimes draw additional vehicles and men from one of the armoured regiments stationed there. Apart from the valuable lessons of experiencing command at an early age, there was the invaluable chance to broaden one's mind and knowledge of one's fellow men on attachments with regular soldiers during vacations.

* * *

Many of us worked hard and by the time the examinations for our commissions came round our military education was quite thorough. Nevertheless, one is always liable to little errors and omissions on the day. An enormous and highly realistic sand table was laid out in the drill-hall at Yeomanry House and as part of the exam, each candidate was invited to solve some tactical problem with the aid of a superb collection of dinky toys. I was asked to describe and demonstrate the procedure for setting up a road block with a troop of armoured cars. I went through all the preparations in great detail and positioned the vehicles with great care on the sand table with due regard for dead ground and the line of the road. I then went through all the procedural points, ticking them off the list in my mind and expecting to be dismissed with a good mark. However, the examining Major kept on asking questions and was clearly unhappy about something. He asked me to go through it all again, but still he wasn't happy. I declared myself baffled at what I might have overlooked. Finally, he leant across the sand table and asked me:

"Would you agree that this would be an improvement?" As he did this he deftly turned the dinky toys around so that the guns faced the enemy rather than our own side. "Oh, yes Sir." I agreed emphatically, at which he looked up for inspiration from the heavens and awarded full marks.

Later that day, the presiding Major was not so lucky. The final event was a series of lectures delivered by each candidate to his fellows and the assembled board. Last on the list was another John Slater, a superb actor who did a popular cabaret act at college balls and who is now a successful barrister. His subject was ".30 Browning Machine-gun Stoppages." He went on at length and with great gusto about what to do if your machine gun jams with a thousand slit-eyed Chinese charging your position. He went through all the drills thoroughly but brought to the demonstration all his well rehearsed cabaret techniques, most of his audience was in near hysterics, including the examining board. At the end he asked for questions. No one had any, but as a matter of form the presiding Major had to ask one.

"What would your immediate action have been if the breech block had been wrongly inserted back to front?" He asked.

John wasn't thrown one bit by this interruption to his act.

"This is a lecture on stoppages" he replied, "if the breech block had been put in back to front the machine gun wouldn't have started in the first place. Next question please!"

* * *

The climax of each training year was the two week annual camp during which the whole O.T.C. trained together, often with another O.T.C. which during my time was Glasgow and Strathclyde University O.T.C. By the end of the two weeks one had generally worked quite hard, learnt a lot and felt a great deal more confident in one's military abilities, but things were not always done strictly by the book.

One camp on Salisbury Plain saw the O.T.C. split into two opposing forces for an escape and evasion exercise. The escapers were to be taken in a landing craft from Poole Harbour to St Austell Bay in Cornwall, where they would be discharged onto a beach and using their initiative had to make their way to the Jamaica Inn on Bodmin moor. The other side knew the landing place and also had the advantage of several vehicles and men with which to capture the escapers. Two of the latter felt that the odds were unfairly stacked against them and therefore hatched a scheme which involved a contribution of £1 from each of their fellows on the attractive promise of a comfortable and foolproof means of escape. For reasons of security no further details were given and spirits sank in the landing craft as they came into St. Austell Bay and saw through binoculars that the landing beach was ringed with the opposing side. It seemed a hopeless situation. Suddenly, however, a very ancient Cornish bus appeared on the road down to the beach. The waiting force had not dared or thought to stop it and as the craft grounded everybody sprinted through the surf and up the beach into the bus. Immediately the bus was off up the narrow Cornish lanes and since it was a hot July day and the roads were busy, the pursuers, when they finally realised what had happened, had little chance of getting in front. It was a joy to look out of the back window to see a string of army vehicles quite unable to pass until the whole group arrived in complete comfort and safety at the Jamaica Inn.

* * *

We had some very good camps at Sennybridge in Wales. It is delightful and wild countryside and many an afternoon waiting for the enemy was spent on one's back in brilliant sunshine watching the buzzards wheel overhead. The weather could be pretty foul up there too and on such a day we received a visit from Major-General d'Avigdor-Goldsmid. It was time for lunch and I stopped in thick mist on a mountain top to have some sandwiches and the bottles of beer which I and my driver had stuffed into the ammunition racks inside our Ferret. It was a time when the army was making great efforts to cut down on traffic accidents by severe penalties for drunken driving. I was in the driver's seat with a bottle of beer actually in my mouth when this head and shoulders wearing a general's red tabs peered in through the driver's hatch to ask how much I enjoyed the army. I don't remember our brief conversation. He then went over to Charles Townshend, who stands a good six and a half feet tall and is endowed with an ultra academic mind. The general was the epitome of a pragmatic soldier.

"How tall are you?"

"I don't really know Sir, it's a long time since I was measured."

"How long have you been in the O.T.C.?"

"I'm not quite sure, Sir, about a year or two, I think, perhaps."

"Do you enjoy it?"

"I don't really know. I suppose I do. I've never thought about it very much."

"You're rather a VAGUE person, aren't you?"
"I don't really know Sir, I've never given it much thought really, I

suppose I might be."

Generals shouldn't suddenly appear out of thick Welsh mists looking for trouble.

* * *

That Saturday, we had a free day and a group of us decided to go hunting on the river Teifi with the Hawkestone Otterhounds. The reader will understand that most participants in this sport either wear a neat scarlet and blue uniform with knee-breeches, or else appear to be hewn out of swathes of solid tweed. Most of us had reasonably suitable clothes but John Slater, the lecturer, was as ever the joker in the pack. He had arrived at Sennybridge straight from a fancy dress party in London to which he had gone as Wyatt Earp. He professed that he had no other clothes to wear. His outfit consisted of a pair of wide leather chaps, tooled and with silver rivets, an elaborately embroidered waistcoat under a black bolero, the whole set off by a flaming neckerchief. Thus it was that he appeared at the meet and plunged into the Teifi in lively pursuit of the otter before the startled doyens of the hunt.

* * *

Beside the square at our camp there was a burnt out hut and going through the remains one night we came across an old but undamaged piano. With the addition of a few drawing pins in the keys it produced a very fine approximation to a honky-tonk. We were due to leave camp the next day on a four day exercise in the surrounding mountains. With great stealth we manhandled the piano across the square in the dark to a three ton truck which was to be one of our support vehicles. With some difficulty we managed to lift it on board and hid it under some blankets and boxes of rations. We also put a well-stocked bar on board. Unless we were in a tactical situation this truck would join the troops of scout cars in their leaguers on the hillsides or in harbour areas in woods. John Slater was a very accomplished pianist capable of spirited renderings of anything from the Rolling Stones to the Moonlight Sonata. Whenever we stopped for long enough he would throw back the tarpaulin on the truck, clear the piano of its disguise and start to play. The bar would open and everybody had a great sing song. Alarmed birds would clatter out of the woods and even the sheep would stop eating and stare in dumb amazement if this performance took place on some deserted hillside. As mentioned earlier, our partners in this camp were from Glasgow and Strathclyde, in the main rather dour Scotsmen who took themselves and their soldiering very seriously. Some among them had little time for the English and the cavalrymen of Oxford represented to them all that was most effete and intolerable. Above all, Glasgow and Strathclyde treasured their pipe band and at the end of every exercise they would march proudly back to camp behind it. This was, of course, a wholly admirable practice and until now Oxford had nothing to match it.

In order to increase the number of scout cars for this annual camp we had collected a dozen second world war Daimler Dingos from a depot on Salisbury Plain. These were magnificent military antiques which required two days mechanical overhaul on arrival at Sennybridge and between one and six hours maintenance a day to keep them running. Most of them had taken the coastal road from Cairo to Berlin twenty years previously but we managed to keep most of them going. They were great fun, and with a little coaxing and tampering with the governors, could be made to do 60 or 70 miles an hour. I heard a rumour that after we had finished with them they were given a fresh coat of paint and sold to an Arab army at £12,000 a piece. If this was true the Arabs would have had no hope of keeping them going in such dusty conditions with their massive maintenance requirement.

When the four day exercise finally ended Glasgow and Strathclyde, feeling very pleased with themselves, fell in behind their band and marched up the long hill to the square to the skirl of the pipes. We watched this performance from afar with every confidence in our plan. As soon as the pipes struck down and the Scotsmen were on the point of being dismissed, we went into action. The three ton truck, with the tarpaulin rolled right back to reveal the piano at its tail end, tore up the hill at top speed, John Slater playing "The Campbells are coming" for all he was worth. The truck was followed by the roar of twelve dingos, backfiring as they tore up the hill in low gear and the dingos were followed by the high pitched whine of the six Ferrets. The nineteen vehicles completed a tour of the square and halted in perfect formation opposite to the Scotsmen with the piano truck out in front in the corresponding position to the pipe band. Engines switched off simultaneously and the only remaining sound was the piano playing "Greensleeves" as we de-kitted the vehicles.

A massive Scottish sense of humour failure was visible across the square.

* * *

It was not all frivolity though, for during this camp Chris Durrant from Kenya and myself were also getting ourselves fit for our forthcoming Parachute Courses. Most evenings we forced ourselves to go on grueling runs in the mountains around, scattering bewildered sheep as we went. I was already very fit from modern Pentathlon but the parachute selection course had a very tough reputation. Chris and I went straight on from Wales to Aldershot where our fellow candidates turned out to be a fine bunch of recruits from a Glasgow parachute engineer regiment. These youngsters turned out to be utterly unbeatable in any circumstances. They had undergone a two week preparation for the selection tests and Chris and I joined them for these the next day.

By eight o'clock we were in full kit, boots and helmets, on a three mile run into Aldershot. When we arrived the first test was of boxing known as 'milling'. In this there are no rules, bar hits below the belt, and the contestants have to stand with their toes touching and are not allowed to move their feet. The idea is to find out whether a man can be aggressive to order, and sustain it. Each contest lasts a minute and a half and you just keep punching the chap opposite until the whistle goes. It is amazing how exhausted you are at the end. We paired off according to size and weight and I picked a thirty five year old with tattoos which started on his left knuckles, went up his left arm, across his chest and down to his right hand. He looked as he had spent a lifetime stirring bar brawls in all the corners of the world. Unfortunately the result of our fight was judged indeterminate and we had to perform again, by the end of which we were absolutely shattered.

At the start we heard the regular para sergeants whispering for who was to have the privilege of taking on "the young gentlemen from Oxford", it was a little like casting lots for Christ's robe. I drew one of the recruits, luckily, but Chris was too tall and big for any of them. The sergeants rubbed their hands with glee and the one who was elected to fight Chris agreed with his fellows that this big fellow would be slow on his feet and would go down with a mighty crash onto the canvas. After a few seconds the horror on the Sergeant's face was joy to behold as he realised his mistake. He came out of the ring a very shaken man. Chris was the light heavyweight in the Oxford University Boxing team.

We then ran a couple of miles in full kit again to a clearing in the woods known as the "Confidence Area". Here there was an elaborate aerial assault course constructed in the trees about twenty feet above the ground. It consisted of crooked planks, ropes, posts and jumps across wide gaps with only a post or narrow plank on the take off and landing sides. Unless these were taken at a good run there was no hope of getting across and there were no safety nets. Since many of the planks were fixed at angles it was difficult to get a good run and the whole course was constructed way up in the trees. The pièce de résistance of this elaborate jungle gym scheme were two towers sixty feet high with two ten foot scaffolding poles between them at their highest point. The poles were parallel, about eighteen inches apart. The would-be para had to climb the tower and then shuffle across the poles standing absolutely upright. When he reached the middle he would be ordered to halt, and to repeat his name, rank and number. If he did this with sufficient confidence he could go on and climb down the other side. All this was designed to test one's confidence and determination and the tests were probably very effective in this.

When we finished this we were feeling quite pleased with ourselves. We had failed to notice, however, another assault course on the ground. This was of the usual type with ropes, ramps, walls, crawling wire and pipes, water splashes and so on. It was not so much a long course as a tough one with many obstacles in a small area. It is far better to have long gaps between obstacles where some muscles can be rested while running. We were given a pep-talk beforehand and told this was the last item on the programme and we had to put everything we had into it. We shot off at a cracking pace and fairly sprinted round. The fitter members of each team always help the less fit and agile at the harder obstacles. When we finished and collapsed on the ground with our heads reeling, our stomachs retching and stars before eyes, we were ordered onto our feet again and told to go round again. We obliged and shot round once more. We thought that must be it now, but no, we were enjoined to go round once more for the Queen. Once more we shot round at a cracking pace our minds by this time hardly attached to our bodies. We had five minutes rest and then an officer told us that our trucks were waiting round the corner of the wood to take us home. We all jumped up full of hope. He hadn't told a lie, the trucks were there. What he omitted to tell us was that between us and the trucks, which we couldn't see, was yet another assault course through the wood. Except for the milling, we had not been out of our full kit with boots and helmets all morning and by this stage we were pretty exhausted. All the time, the regular staff were screaming, brandishing sticks and letting off blank rounds and thunderflashes. This final assault course was pure bedlam and the orders were each man for himself. At the end we were ordered to sprint for the trucks. On emerging from the wood we saw them. Half a mile away!

Fortunately Chris and I, as undergraduates, had had both the time and opportunity to get extremely fit. Many of the Glasgow lads, however, had really only had their two weeks to get fit in and I think probably had a harder time of it than we did. As soon as the back of the truck went up though, someone burst into song with "Oh, ye canna shove your Granny off a bus," and the whole truck joined in as we sped back to camp. They were absolutely irrepressible.

* * *

The camps and the courses were naturally the high points of O.T.C. life. But apart from these there was training most weekends and one weekday evening as well. This was not devoid of amusement either. We had one or two certifiable cases in our number including a notorious undergraduate who with great difficulty managed to get a driving licence through the army. One day he was under instruction in a ferret, as they approached a neatly kept roundabout. The commander ordered "straight over here" through the headsets and the character did just that. He drove straight off the road, up one side of the grass roundabout, across the flower beds, flattened two silver birch trees and down the other side back onto the road.

* * *

One of the great opportunities offered by the O.T.C. was the chance to train in exotic overseas stations with regular regiments. And so it was that in 1967 I flew out to Benghazi in Libya to join the 5th Royal Inniskilling Dragoon Guards, which regiment I was subsequently to join as a reservist and to follow around the globe. In those days there was a small British contingent in Libya at the invitation of King Idris.

An armoured reconnaissance regiment, less one squadron, a platoon of Infantry and some staff in Benghazi, an airfield at EL Adem outside Tobruk and a troop of Royal Engineers under a sergeant somewhere in the four hundred miles between. There can be few stations nowadays in which a regiment can live its own life so far from its headquarters, which in this case was in Malta.

The regiment was accommodated in the huts of Wavell Camp on the outskirts of Benghazi towards Benina airfield. The Officers' Mess and the extensive stables were in a barracks in the town, known as Newmarket. The Mess building had originally been an Italian Army Corporals' Mess but had since gone through many changes of military proprietors. The Libyan army, or Cyrenaican Defence Force had most of the barracks next door. While the place had been in German hands during the war, David Stirling and his Special Air Service had raided it, climbing over the wall behind our Mess. There were two fine palm trees in a small garden in front of the Newmarket Mess, diligently watered by an almost sightless Arab.

For the soldier this part of North Africa is full of memories. The ground was fought over many times in the Second World War as the fortunes of either side ebbed and flowed. The desert is full of relics - burnt out vehicles, a few uncleared minefields but mostly smaller reminders like rusting cans of bully beef and 'Benghazi cookers', testaments to 'brews' of long ago. The areas of empty desert where we exercised formerly bore names such as "Knightbridge" and were seldom absent from the front pages of newspapers in the early years of that war. Perhaps the most obvious legacy of that chapter of world history is the abundance of old uniforms still worn by the Arabs, British army greatcoats being a great status symbol, but the axis forces by no means neglected - a particularly disconcerting sight being our gardener who wandered about his parched flower beds in pajamas trousers and a Wehrmacht corporal's tunic.

Libya is a fascinating and stimulating country. It has, of course, a magnificent beach the whole length of its coastline. Behind this are some of the finest and most impressive Greek and Roman remains to be found anywhere. Behind these ruins at Cyrene, Ptolemaida, Leptis Magna, and Sabratha lies the desert, which will always exert its own fascination on the British. Some parts of Libya are extremely fertile, such as the areas around Barce and Tripoli and there are the attractive hills of the Jebel Akdar. Everywhere, from the Cathedral of Tripoli and the Opera House in Benghazi, to the settler's homesteads of the plain of Barce, are signs of later Italian efforts to restore the country to its significance of 2000 years ago. Now of course, Libya, has found that significance again through the unexpected medium of oil.

As far as soldiering was concerned, the Libyan desert was an ideal training ground. There was plenty of room to practice the skills of armoured warfare without doing any harm or damage. However far one went into the desert it never seemed long before an Arab turned up. Sleeping in a ferret miles from anywhere there would be a knock on the turret at dawn. Throwing it open, one discovered an Arab clutching a basket — "Eggs, Tommy?"

I arrived during the last week of spring rain. Exercising in this was rather like driving round the car park at the average English point to point. The sand quickly became waterlogged and one was apt to become deeply bogged down in vivid orange mud. The difficulties of the First Army in Western Tunisia in 1943 could be well imagined. The following week, however, was sheer delight. Along the coast of Libya runs an escarpment of between four and eight hundred feet, and between half a mile and ten miles from the sea. South of Benghazi there is a coastal plain about five miles wide and one morning we crossed this to go up the escarpment and beyond. During this week after the rains all the flowers come out for a few days before the hot sun proves too much and they burn and shrivel to disappear for another year. The drive across the plain remains a most vivid memory. To say it was like driving over a carpet may not be avoiding a cliché, but there is no other way to describe the profusion and variety of purples, blues, yellows and reds of the flowers. In an open scout car the perfume was almost overwhelming. We climbed the escarpment to look down on a slightly threadbare, but vivid carpet as far as the eye could see.

* * *

Opportunities for soldiering were superb, and there were facilities for all the usual sports, but nevertheless the opportunities for night life were limited. There were 'dinner nights' in the Mess three or four nights a week at which the fine silver was displayed to advantage in this exotic setting. With superb food and wine and cards or backgammon afterwards the lack of outside entertainment could be tolerated. One officer specialised in pre-dinner drinks trips in his Maserati up to the rundown bar at the top of the Tocra Pass and back at an average speed approaching a hundred miles an hour. There were a couple of night clubs in Benghazi, one of which, the Riviera, had recently opened. Three of us went along one night, taking with us a great stock of booze in our pockets and under our jackets, since whisky was £24 a bottle in the club. We ordered three coca colas at £1 each and chose a discreet table at which to consume our illicit supply. The place was full of single Arabs and some European hostesses who were totally unresponsive but might have been if we had bought them some of those bottles of whisky. The cabaret was extremely good and when a very talented stripper came on we moved down to a table at the front, leaving a great pile of empty bottles under our table. Just as she finished her act there was a great roar of rage behind us and we turned to see an enormous negro on his hands and knees rummaging through the empties under our previous table. He picked up a handful and started to cross the floor towards us brandishing the evidence. Out of the corners of my eyes I could see other Arabs running towards the main doors to cut off our retreat. "Let's go" someone said and we sprinted for the door. We just made it. I wouldn't give much for our chances if we hadn't. Our Fiat 500 parked outside carried the three of us off as fast as it could.

* * *

Less than six weeks after I left Libya the Arab-Israeli war of 1967 broke out and there were agitated riots in Benghazi and Tripoli. The regiment put into action a contingency plan and evacuated almost the whole European population of Benghazi within the wire perimeter of Wavell Camp and a thousand or so extra people sweated it out for two weeks in the tin huts. Some members of the regiment were badly burned inside their vehicles in the town. Newmarket was held by one officer and a Mess waiter, each armed with a sub-machine gun. A platoon of the Cyrenaican Defence Force took up positions between the tennis court and the palm trees. The plan of defence was that in the event of an attack, one of the two would sit on the roof squirting, while the other nipped over the wall at the back and hoofed it.

* * *

When I came down from Oxford a year later, I was to return to Libya with a friend for a more thorough tour of its antiquities. This too was a conspicuously successful visit, which got off to an auspiciously imperial start as we were rowed out in a bumboat in the evening sun to join our ship at anchor in the Grand Harbour in Valletta. By now the British army had left Benghazi and shortly after our visit violence again broke out in the coup which brought Ghaddafi to power. Friends with whom we stayed in Tripoli narrowly escaped. Apart from our explorations of the ruins, one highlight of this trip was a visit to the keeper of the King's Bees. This was a redoubtable English lady, who, may I be forgiven for writing, must have been in her eighties, and farmed on her own at Ras-el-Hilal between Appollonia and Derna. She was a legend in her own time. The first day we turned up at her immaculate farm, quite the best we had seen in the whole of Libya. Mustapha, her house-boy, received us and told us she was seeing the King in Beida. He asked us to come back the next day and as we left picked a magnificent bunch of grapes off a vine, ready wrapped in an airmail copy of 'The Times' for visitors. We took the news of her visit to the King with a pinch a salt but later found this to be unjustified. She had been brought by King Idris from Jordan, where she had also been keeper of the King's Bees, for a transfer fee which would shame many a top-class footballer. She became a great favourite of Idris, with whom she was contemporaneous, and not only did she regularly advise him on government Agricultural Policy, but at least two Ministers owed their dismissals to her advice. What is more, I have no doubt that it was good advice, for she ran a very fine farm.

The next day we went back and were received by a deceptively frail looking and elderly Englishwoman. We were invited inside the house, which, like most of the good buildings in Libya, passed through many hands during the war. The Italians and later the Germans had a brigade headquarters in the house at various periods, and during the latter's occupation one of the soldiers had evidently been a very talented cartoonist. For above the centre pages from the Illustrated London News of the Royal Family complete with corgis at Balmoral, were a series of remarkable wall paintings. All the wartime leaders were there, including most of the German Generals in North Africa. The Allied leaders were there too, painted without a trace of malice. Indeed, the central figure was Churchill, a great bulldog pose with the famous cigar and 'V' sign.

We went out onto the terrace to be shown the cobras, puff-adders and horned vipers coiled up under the rose bushes below. We hadn't noticed them before and began to feel a little uneasy. Our hostess wasn't the least bit put out. "Had to chase two cobras out of the dining room last night before I could start dinner." She added. The farm was in fact a magnet for snakes who could find more to eat there than in the desert. They apparently followed her water-course down out of the desert, and for this reason were more poisonous than usual. Apparently the more barren the desert, the more poisonous the snakes.

We stayed for dinner that night and had a most interesting conversation. I am afraid that our hostess belonged to a different era though. Simply because we were from Oxford she assumed that we would have the contacts to perform a number of diplomatic coups on her, and the Libyan's, behalf. Perhaps in days of more restricted entry to the Foreign Office and Parliament our ilk might have been able to oblige her. After dinner we sat on armchairs taken out by the houseboys onto the terrace, but not before taking a discreet look for horned vipers under the cushions first.

A feature of this visit was the extreme heat. When we arrived in Benghazi on the ship it was 109° F in the shade and very humid. Now, a hot wind like a blow lamp was blowing out of the desert. Normally it would carry sand and form a sand-storm, but now it was just relentlessly hot, for three days on end. I remember trying to shave at 8 a.m. by the old airfield on the Tobruk road above Derna. My shaving brush was dry before I could get it to my face.

A year later we were privileged to take this remarkable old lady out to dinner in London, after she too had been thrown out by the new order in Libya.

CHAPTER EIGHT

TWO WEEKS BEFORE THE MAST

Vacations were an important part of Oxford life, in theory at least one was supposed to use them for preparation of work for the coming term. I always did this, rather against my better judgement, since it was never so interesting to go over the work a second time during the term and familiarity bred contempt. Much of my vacation time was also spent in doing courses and training with the army, but a student of modern languages always has a ready pretext for swanning off abroad.

During my first year I had a most splendid motorcar of the same vintage as myself, 1946, a dark green MG TC. It was complete in every way and was a real collector's piece. Unfortunately I had to choose later on between keeping this magnificent car and buying a polo pony and having been offered a much higher price than I bought it for, I chose the horse and sold the car to an American. I believe it is now in Chicago. Had I kept the car another six or seven years I could have bought several polo ponies with the proceeds. I rather think that several American syndicates were operating in Britain at that time buying up these cars, since one hardly sees any nowadays and at the time I sold mine they were fetching four or five times my selling price on the West coast of the States. Mine was in excellent condition and original in every detail.

It was a great temptation to tour in this car in Europe during the summer and so during my first long vacation I set off with a friend from Oriel for the South. It was only when we arrived on the cross-channel ferry that David and I realised that tomorrow was the 14th July, Bastille Day, and we changed our plans accordingly in order to take in the celebrations in Paris. After watching the parade down the Champs Elysées we left the car outside Notre-Dame and had a look round inside. It was only when we emerged from the Cathedral that I realised what a draw the car was. For there, outside the Cathedral was an American writhing in ecstasy over the bonnet, drooling over the headlights and radiator and gasping in profound wonder as we fed him titbits about the car's history. The upshot of this was that in deference to my choice of carriage he put us up for three days in his apartment round the corner.

Paris, is of course, a very good place to be on Bastille Day and we wandered along the banks of the Ile de la Cité refusing the various substances offered to us by the hippies, and from time to time David would earn our conversational keep playing and singing on the nearest guitar. In those days this was where the hippies congregated and it made a pleasant stroll so long as one was careful to step over 'the bad trips'. Now they have all been cleared away in the interest of a better class of tourist. After watching the splendid fireworks display reflected in the Seine and silhouetting the rooves of the western end of the Ile de la Cité, we repaired to the Place de la Contrescarpe. To the eyes of the reserved Anglo-Saxon this presented an amazing sight. The whole square throbbed and was alive with dancing people. Newcomers kept flooding in and immediately started to dance with complete strangers. Various cabarets were going on around the square including one male stripper, followed by two complete drunks, which brought great guffaws of approval from the crowd.

After a few days in Paris, we left for Chartres and a tour of the Loire châteaux and later found ourselves at the calanques east of Marseille. A few more days here and we decided to head for Spain. We were just driving through the dock area of Marseille when a car with two women in overtook us and stayed level with us. At first I thought they were a couple of insistent filles de joie, and was just commenting to David that mine was alright but I didn't much fancy his, when the younger girl leant out and addressed us in English. The car, it seemed, had done it once again. The other occupant of the car, who turned out to be the girl's mother, extended an invitation to us to come and stay at their seaside house. Of course we accepted. They had a charming house at an exclusive small resort west of Marseille and we were entertained. They took us to their beach club and sailing in the bay, where we caught a glimpse of the great lamp-bracket jowl and expressive grin of Fernandel, fishing at anchor offshore.

Later that night we went to the casino, where they insisted on a minimum age of 21 when I asked to play. David, who was unconventionally dressed in patchy jeans and the brim, but not the main substance of a straw boater, gave his age as 23 and the cashier reluctantly handed over his chips. He looked David up and down with disgust as he did so and finally leant over, took the straw boater brim off his head and with audible disgust threw it into a waste paper basket. David became very indignant at this and we started to create such a row that the cashier was finally induced to pick the brim out of the basket and replace it on David's head, averting his gaze as he did so. Meanwhile the croupiers, who were completely unoccupied, as no one else was playing the tables, had been amusing themselves by creating intricate patterns and constructions with the chips. They registered absolute disgust at the prospect of such a player and they reluctantly dismantled their amusements and rearranged the chips on the tables ready for play. There then followed a grotesque scene. I had explained the rudiments of the game to David, who had only wanted to play when he saw me turned away. I situated myself between two palm trees on the edge of the playing area, which was as close as a minor was allowed, and directed his play. Between each throw the game was halted as David walked over to me to ask advice on the next move. The croupiers could hardly believe it. Still less so when my weak system triumphed ultimately to the tune of one Franc and we retired, the point having been made. The cashier thumped his machine as he changed our chips back and with a contemptuous sneer flicked our one Franc winnings across his counter. We collected it with effusive thanks and returned to the dance.

* * *

After a brief stay with some friends from Cambridge, who were teaching water skiing on the Costa Brava, we struck out for the interior of Spain. Early one morning at about 7 a.m. we were descending a mountain pass the other side of Lerida towards Zaragoza. In my rear view mirror I suddenly caught sight of a Mini-moke with British registration plates bearing down on us, with arms and legs protruding from every opening. There was no other traffic about and we raced with them down the pass, overtaking each other on hideous bends. Finally when we were ahead, we stopped for breakfast an hour later. They stopped too, thinking we might have broken down, and joined our meal. There were five of them, including two Old Marlburians and an attractive blonde. We all seemed to be going the same way so we agreed to travel together. After a leisurely lunch break the other side of Zaragossa, we decided to race for Toledo that night. We arrived in Madrid during the rush hour and by now we were slightly ahead. Madrid has many broad boulevards with the central reservations neatly planted with flowers and box-hedges. We shot up one of these and realised we were going the wrong way. We came to a gap and did a "U" turn onto the other carriageway.

The others had followed us and when they saw us hammering down the opposite side of the boulevard, they simply drove straight at the central reservation, and crashed through the flowers and box-hedges, as amazed Spaniards hooted, swore and swerved to avoid them. When we arrived in Toledo we turned up a track and found a flat piece of ground to sleep on. Exhausted, we went straight to sleep. When we woke at six the next morning, we saw rats all around us. In the dark we had chosen to camp in Toledo municipal rubbish dump.

* * *

In Toledo the crew of the Moke invited us to go with them to Portugal, where the father of one of them owned a hotel in Estoril. We thought very hard about this offer, but regretfully had to turn it down, as we were getting short of money and had decided to head straight for Gibraltar, where we hoped to get a job of some sort. After a pause to read about Chairman Mao's swim in 'The Times' on the beach at Marbella, we arrived at the Spanish customs in La Linea. In those days the frontier was still open, but cars were delayed for a varying period each day. This day we were lucky, about 20 minutes per car. The little customs man went through everything, sticking wires in our petrol tanks, looking through our toolbox and all the while consulting his watch to see how much longer he had to protract the pantomime. We found it all quite diverting and finally he came across some books I had with me in preparation for the coming term. He pulled out a copy of Voltaire's "Zaire"

"Que Es?" he enquired, waving it in the air.

"Pornografia!" I replied, giving a knowing leer.

"Ah!" the delighted little man cried in excitement and dashed into his office to check it against the list with which he was provided of sought after titles in this branch of literature. We felt genuinely sorry for him when he couldn't find it on the list, as he so clearly desired promotion.

"A matter for headquarters" he said, and dialed a number on the telephone attached to the wall. We watched him through the glass of his office spelling out the name of the book and the author, shrugging his shoulders and them finally turning a vivid red. I don't suppose the

Spanish muck about with their police and customs very much. A joke was something quite new. He slammed down the receiver and curtly handed over the book, waving us on our way.

When we arrived at the Gibraltar Immigration they didn't believe us when we gave as our proposed address that of the Colonial Secretary. We looked very dirty and scruffy. In fact the Colonial Secretary and his family were acquaintances of David's and after a telephone call to check our story, here too we were waved on our way - this time with very smart salutes from three of the Gibraltar Customs Officers. I hope the little Spaniard was watching.

* * *

Soon we were sipping drinks on the terrace of their charming house, surrounded by oleander and bougainvillea and looking across the Straits to the hills of Morocco. We explained our plans of finding a job to ease our financial position and asked if we could leave the car in their garage if we managed to find a job on a yacht. After half an hour of walking round the yacht pens we found a yacht needing crew for a month's round trip to Majorca. We could hardly believe our luck. In fact Gibraltar is quite a good place to pick up work, as for many yachts setting out from Britain for Mediterranean and Caribbean cruises, Gibraltar is the first port of call. By this time they may have had a difficult storm in the Bay of Biscay, or at least long enough for the complements to find out if they get on with each other or not. Many crews leave or are exchanged wholesale between skippers. We should perhaps have been warned. To clinch the deal we agreed to pay £4 a week for our keep in view of our inexperience. This was better than spending that much on petrol alone each day driving the car around.

When we got on board everything seemed very pleasant. It was a beautiful 38 ½ ton two masted yacht with fine lines, built in 1914 for a French count. Down below all was magnificent teak and the saloon was complete with panelling and a tiled coal fireplace. The present owner was a retired R.A.F. Officer, sailing with his wife back to his native New Zealand. All seemed very pleasant as we sat in the cockpit in Gibraltar enjoying the evening sun. As the days went by we were a little puzzled not to have sailed already, as per the original agreement, but set about the various jobs we were asked to do. We realised later there two reasons

83

for this - first the skipper had a paying crew he could use to do all the maintenance on his boat and second, he was almost incapable of taking any decisions at all, especially on when, or when not to sail. Whichever way he did not decide, he would pace about cursing his ill-luck and imagining conspiracies against him. During our pause in the yacht-pens we were joined by Anne, the young wife of an R.A.F. officer who was going away for three weeks, and one night by the most polished sponger I have ever seen. He was utterly charming and invited himself to dinner with experienced ease. He went on at length about high life in Gibraltar and didn't seem amused when David and I pointed out that he could eat his fill for 4/8 d at "Smokey Joe's" and get his passport endorsed with a stamp saying "Eat at Smokey Joe's" as well. This stamp was invariably put on the same page as any Spanish endorsements and caused no end of trouble.

When we finally sailed from Gibraltar we began to realise what sort of boat we were on. The drinks stopped and food was strictly rationed. The skipper was appallingly rude to his rather stupid wife, who must have been beaten into submission years ago. He was a colonial with a mighty chip on his shoulder – "My father sweated for the improvement of farmland in New Zealand and now the blasted Maori says 'Thank you very much, I want it back.' I then served Britain in two ways, I faced the bullets to save it from fascist jackboot and I subsidized its economy with my taxes! And what thanks did I get? Nothing! I am going back to New Zealand" etc. etc. etc. ad nauseam. I would describe my own politics as fairly conservative but this man was ridiculous. I admit that we amused ourselves by encouraging him into absurd extremist views and, in Malaga, by bringing copies of the "New Statesman" on board, a publication which I do not normally read out of choice. These we left lying around prominently. He must in fact have been the original Brylcreem boy for he would spend up to 20 minutes each morning applying the substance and combing his locks in the mirror. Vanity was also apparent in his naked torso as he strode around the yacht on the chilliest nights.

He was a pretty incompetent sailor too - his main preoccupation on entering harbour was to see that all was beautifully polished and varnished and that the right flags were put up - meanwhile he would disappear below to comb his hair only to re-emerge to issue frantic contradictory orders as we were about to crash into the quayside.

He would then blame his wife, Anne, David and myself - anyone but himself. It wasn't worth pointing out that he was being subsidized for his crew's admitted inexperience. I often think that many sailors cast off into a dream world of their own to escape realities. This one certainly did and he got very upset when reality demonstrated that he couldn't have it all his own way.

David and I soon resolved that there was no point in getting worked up or remonstrating with this totally unreasonable man. The minus side was obvious, but on the plus side we were saving ourselves a lot of money, and the sailing could be absolutely superb. We would cruise along in a fine breeze sunning ourselves on the deck, or trailing our toes in the water watching the schools of dolphins which periodically followed our course and played around the yacht. Flying fish would dart across the deck or strand themselves on it and we would toss them back in. The weather was good and we were seeing a lot of new places. We decided not to react in any way but to let our skipper fume at his leisure. We would ride this horse as long as it suited us. Our problem was Anne, whom we were careful not to influence in any way, but we could see she was not happy with the situation. If we jumped ship she would be in a very awkward position.

Perhaps he worked on the old maxim, "bullshit baffles brains" - as long as everything looking alright, it was alright. A good example of this and his manners was the spinnaker which we discovered while clearing out the fo'csle. It obviously hadn't been inspected for months and was completely rotten, covered in black mould and holes starting to appear everywhere.

"Oh crikey, some idiot must have packed it away without looking at it. That's £300 down the drain, oh crikey."

We advised him to throw it out before it spread to the other sails but he told us to pack it back into the fo'csle, out of sight.

Similarly in Malaga. About five quayside workers were delivering water onto the boat and our skipper, pretending to put the hose into the water inlet let as much as possible run over the decks to clean them, thereby wasting a good deal of the docker's time.

"Let the bastards wait" he said and went downstairs to save water another way by having a shower. Poetic justice was meted out by a flood which streamed out of every washbasin and lavatory on the boat as airlocks developed.

His wife was not much more generous. There was never enough milk for breakfast cereal. Neither was there enough tea to go round and she hoped that if she didn't pour any out for you, you wouldn't bother to ask for any.

Things came to a head in Alicante. One of the other yachtsmen in the harbour pointed out that our masts needed varnishing very badly. The crew of a yacht next door whispered across to us that it would take at least six days to do the mizzen alone. We felt that we were not paying £4 each a week to sit around in harbours doing routine maintenance, so when our skipper asked us to do this job we naturally refused.

A second incident really did the trick. After we had crashed into the quayside in our normal manner, while our immaculate poseur screamed abuse at all and sundry, we finally managed to tie up end-on to the quay. The next day a small French yacht came in on sail alone. It did a beautifully timed turn as it approached the quay, dropped its anchor and slid in backwards with enviable precision. David remarked to our skipper what good form this manoeuvre had been.

"Good form!" he screamed "when he's got his chain curled all over ours!" This was certainly not the case. David and I caught a couple of ropes they threw us and later the two of us and Anne were invited on board this new neighbour for drinks. Our hosts turned out to be the General in charge of the base at Mers-El-Kebir in Algeria, his A.D.C. and a legionnaire subaltern. They were charming and showed us round their yacht. In return we said we would ask if they could have a look round ours, particularly in view of its fine saloon and French connections.

We put this to our skipper. It was quite evident that what riled him was that his crew had been hobnobbing it with the generals next door and he, saviour of Western Europe from the fascist hordes, had not been included.

"Certainly not!" he said "Why should I give hospitality to someone who has given you hospitality. It would have been different if they had asked US on board. You should never accept hospitality if you can't return it. In fact you're a pair of SCROUNGERS, both of you! - You've scrounged off them and you're scrounging off us."

It was hopeless to reason with such a man, or to point out that he was collecting £8 from us for our keep, in addition to our willing service as crew. Only a psychiatrist could make sense of this man.

It was sheer delight to repeat this story in French next day to the Frenchmen alongside, while our skipper looked on unable to understand a word. The French were hugely amused as we had put them in the picture the night before.

The three of us, David, Anne and I, had now discussed the situation at length and Anne said she wasn't staying with "those two" by herself if we left. When David and I were asked to strip and varnish the masts again we said nothing but simply packed our bags and called a taxi. The driver came on board to collect our bags and we said goodbye.

The problem now was to get back from this corner of Spain to Gibraltar. We started to hitch but it was hopeless. We made 45 miles in the day and waited for hours outside a town called Alcantarilla, which translated means sewer. There was, however, a train which left at 11 pm. for Alcazar, south of Madrid, from where we could get another train next day down to Algeciras. So we entertained the local riffraff on David's guitar until the train left. When we got aboad it was difficult to find anywhere to sit for the journey through the night. The train was full of nursing mothers with children and sailors in spotless white uniforms on leave from Cartagena. As soon as they saw that we were foreigners, babies were thrown off the seats, sailors spread newspapers on the floor and lay down on them and everyone insisted that we sit on the cleared wooden bench. We were highly embarrassed by all this as there was no conceivable reason why these people should be put to all this trouble on our account. However, we were forcibly pressed down on the seats and it would have caused offence to turn down the offer. They really were splendid people.

At 11 a.m. the next morning a very smart train glided into the station at Alcazar de San Juan. We climbed aboard and for the first time felt really scruffy and dirty in the plush seats of this air-conditioned express. Sure enough, a supplement was charged and we sped on south. Slowly we noticed that our travelling companions were all rather silent young couples holding hands. We had intruded on a honeymoon special.

After a fine trip through the gorges and cork forests of the Sierra Ronda we arrived in Algeciras. We were toying with the idea of going straight over to Tangier, but we just missed a ferry and would have had to wait 4 hours for the next. That might not seem a great hardship, but you would understand if you had ever been to Algeciras in high summer. The stench from what sewers there may be is quite indescribable. I suppose it is a good place for honeymoons - it gives you an excuse for staying in your room with the windows shut anyway. Once more we repaired to Gibraltar to the Colonial Secretary's house, where Lady Bates said that she had had reservations all along. In fact she never heard of a crewing job picked up in Gibraltar which worked out satisfactorily.

* * *

Some months later one of the Old Marlburians in the Mini-moke came to my room in Oriel to enter his horse for a race in the Point—to—Point which I was running.

"You know" he started, "you should have come to Portugal with us."

"Oh?" I enquired,

"Yes, you see when we arrived at this chap's father's hotel in Estoril, he took one look at us and paid each of us £5 a day to keep away from his hotel as long as we wanted to stay!"

EPILOGUE

There was an original twist to another holiday some months later. Shortly after coming down from Oxford half a dozen of us were skiing in a tiny and obscure resort in the Southern Alps of France. I spotted two twin girls coming up on the ski lift and quite fancied the look of them. Ten minutes later I was standing still further down the slope when one of them came crashing into me, sending us both flying.

Five years after that we were married. But that is another story.